The Six Days of Destruction
Meditations toward Hope

Elie Wiesel
and
Albert H. Friedlander

Paulist Press
New York/Mahwah

Library of Congress Cataloging-in-Publication Data

Wiesel, Elie, 1928–
    The six days of destruction: meditations toward hope/by Elie Wiesel and Albert H. Friedlander.
      p. cm.
    ISBN 0-8091-0409-1: $9.95   ISBN 0-8091-2999-X (pbk.): $4.95
    1. Holocaust, Jewish (1939–1945)—Fiction.   2. Holocaust
Remembrance Day—Prayer-books and devotions—English.
3. Judaism—Prayer-books and devotions—English.   4. Prayers.
I. Friedlander, Albert H.   II. Title.
PQ2683.I32S5   1988
813'.54—dc19   88-17648
                                                         CIP

Published by Paulist Press
997 Macarthur Boulevard
Mahwah, New Jersey 07430

Printed and bound in the
United States of America

Contents

For my friend
Sigmund

Acknowledgements

The six chronicles of the Holocaust were translated from the original French text by Cynthia Landes and Evelyn Friedlander. The six meditations on Genesis 1:1–31, including the translations of the Biblical text, are the work of the co-author and based upon the King James version.

The Publisher gratefully acknowledges the use of the following materials: "From Death to Hope, Liturgical Reflections on the Holocaust," by Eugene J. Fisher and Leon Klenicki, Copyright © 1983 by Stimulus Foundation. All rights reserved. Used by permission; Music for "Hear, O Israel" by Gregory Norbet, O.S.B., copyright The Benedictine Foundation of the State of Vermont, Inc., Weston Priory, Weston, VT.; Stories excerpted from *Their Brothers' Keepers* by Philip Friedman (New York: Holocaust Library, 1978), by permission of Holocaust Library; Excerpts from *Young Moshe's Diary, The Spiritual Torment of a Jewish Boy in Nazi Europe*, are reprinted by permission of Yad VaShem, Jerusalem; The Kaddish Prayer is reprinted from *Gates of Prayer* (1975), by permission of the copyright holder, Central Conference of American Rabbis and Union of Liberal and Progressive Synagogues, New York; Portions from the Book of Genesis are reprinted from the Jewish Publication Society Bible; English text of "Again the Wagons Wait for Us," (Y. Katzenelson) and "Psalm," (Paul Celan) by Albert H. Friedlander. All rights reserved; "Liturgical Meditation for Our Time," by Albert H. Friedlander. All rights reserved; Excerpts from *Ani Maamin: A Song Lost and Found Again* by Elie Wiesel, translated by Marion Wiesel, are published by permission of Random House,

foreword

Liturgies are also literature, and the Central Conference of American Rabbis has been a pioneer in this field of religious expression. In 1980 it began serious work on *The Five Scrolls*, a prayerbook for the three pilgrim festivals and the holiday of Purim and the solemn day of the Ninth of Av. On each of these holy days, one of the five biblical Scrolls—Ecclesiastes, Esther, Song of Songs, Ruth, Lamentations—is read in the synagogue with appropriate liturgy. During the planning, the suggestion was made that an extra liturgy for Yom Hashoah be attached to Lamentations. The Book of Lamentations was written to lament the destruction of the Temple in Jerusalem, but had not been deemed by tradition to be time-bound to that event. Indeed, it was recited on the Ninth of Av in mourning for many catastrophes in Jewish history. However, the idea was discarded. The Shoah is so distinctive that it requires its own Scroll. The suggestion was then made to add to the book a sixth Scroll, with an appropriate liturgy. This, too, was rejected, on the grounds that the five Scrolls were historically a family; more than that, the Scroll of the Shoah and its liturgy deserved to stand alone, as the Jewish people had stood alone during those years of unspeakable horror at the hands of the Nazis as the world looked on.

There was yet another consideration: this should not be a book for the Jews alone. This catastrophe belongs to the world. All humanity participated in one form or another. Not only Jews were murdered, and not only Christians looked away. We could not expect Christians to utilize a Jewish liturgy of "Six Scrolls" which would observe five particular Jewish festivals and a remembrance day for the Shoah. Yet, we knew of the need for Christendom to come to liturgical grips with the

Shoah, to pour out grief and remorse, repentance and hope. Inquiries of reliable Roman Catholic and Protestant authorities resulted in encouragement, and thus our decision to make *The Six Days of Destruction* available to all.

Whom could we approach who could take on the awesome role of neo-biblical authorship? The answer, obviously, was Elie Wiesel.

Just as obvious was the selection of Albert Friedlander to prepare the liturgy with as full an understanding of the subject matter as is humanly possible and with a sensitivity of which he is so uniquely possessed.

In memory of our Six Million, in sorrow and in hope, we present a new Scroll—*The Six Days of Destruction*.

RABBI JOSEPH B. GLASER
Executive Vice President
Central Conference of American Rabbis

foreword

In a 1979 address to Jewish organizations, Pope John Paul II said that Christians and Jews are "linked together at the very level of their identity." The relationship between our communities, then, is not temporary or superficial, but enduring and deep.

When people are closely related, they cannot remain ignorant of or uncaring about one another. To do so would be to deny part of their very selves. And if it is sad for a person not to know himself or herself, it is tragic for a people to lack that same kind of self-awareness.

On the other hand, to enter into dialogue with one another, to recognize what we share in common, and to acknowledge what is unique to our respective communities enriches and changes us in ways we may not expect.

As peoples of the Book, we Jews and Christians share the conviction that God is at work in our histories, in our lived experiences, in the stories of our successes and failures as well as our joys and sorrows. And our histories, experiences, and stories are still living. They demand our attention and prayerful reflection.

I am happy to have this opportunity to endorse this work of Elie Wiesel and Albert Friedlander. The Shoah, while it is a uniquely Jewish event, also belongs to the entire human family. If we Christians are true to ourselves, then we will acknowledge that the pain and horror of the Holocaust are also ours.

I encourage Christians to reflect upon the contents of this book and to commemorate the Holocaust by means of the liturgy presented here. This will make our relationship with our Jewish sisters and brothers real and authentic.

While we cannot undo the past, we need not and must not repeat it. As Jews and Christians, we must remember it in such a way that the memory shapes our common future in which God and his purposes shall be our sole guide and inspiration.

JOSEPH CARDINAL BERNARDIN
Archbishop of Chicago

foreword

Before I began reading the contents of this book, I had some rather detailed knowledge of its subject and of the author of the six meditations. Nevertheless, I was touched in ways that I could not have imagined.

I see a special significance in the fact that Christians as well as Jews have been invited to add a foreword. For me it is one indication of the distance that Jew and Christian have traveled together in my lifetime. Our thoughts to each other about the most profound events in our histories now have an importance for each other which they have not always had.

Certainly one of the most encouraging developments of recent years has been the closer relations that have occurred between Christians and Jews. After centuries of tragedy, deep misunderstanding and Christian persecutions of Jewish people which remain beyond adequate description or understanding, new appreciations of common roots and shared convictions about social justice and religious freedom have been identified. Christians have acknowledged and sought to repent of their role in this history.

One of the most poignant and sensitive places for Christians and Jews to meet has been in remembrance of, and reflection about, the Holocaust. This book therefore is a special resource not only for Jewish people but also for Christians who wish to meditate on this unparalleled tragedy—the Shoah.

Although its understanding will forever defy human comprehension, no human being living in the last half of the twentieth century can be untouched by the events of the Shoah. No one is better able to speak of the Shoah in a personal context than Elie Wiesel, who encountered and lived through this time of history. Here are six meditations, linked to the Book of Genesis, that speak to Christians as well as Jews as they reflect upon this profound religious and spiritual problem of our century. I have read them all; some I have reread; I have found them all unforgettable. They portray in personal terms a situation which we too often allow to remain abstract.

At the completion of this reading, it is difficult to know what is the appropriate response. For some it will be prayer, for others it will be a recognition that in the light of the Shoah prayer is not possible for them. Those who wish to be in prayer will find the liturgical material that forms the conclusion of the volume to be of value. There is also a helpful word to Christians as to how this material can be used in their own worship.

I strongly recommend to my fellow Christians that they listen to this book's message, meditate upon it, and have the Shoah affect their worship and their lives.

REV. DR. WILLIAM G. RUSCH
Executive Director
Office for Ecumenical Affairs
Evangelical Lutheran Church in America

introduction

Can there be prayers after the Holocaust? Theodor Adorno stated that no poetry could be written after Auschwitz. Prayer is poetry. Each catastrophe of Jewish life—the destruction of the Temple, the blood-baths of the Crusades, the pogroms in Eastern Europe—was followed by an outpouring of Jewish prayers which fixed these events in the liturgy and in the memory of the Jewish people. The confessional prayers of the High Holy Days (slichot); the mourning chants of the Ninth of Av (kinot); the memorial prayers which included the martyrs of all the millennia of Jewish history: this was the poetry of Jewish prayer for the times of darkness.

Then came Auschwitz; and there were many scholars and rabbis who could no longer say the old prayers for the new event. The Holocaust was different. It was unique. The old prayers had given comfort with their assertion that the suffering was part of the Divine Plan, "afflictions of love" (yissurim shel ahavah) through which the children of God were purified. They reminded Jews of their own sins (mipne chatta-eynu) through which they had been exiled from the land and from the nearness of God. They taught acceptance. The Testing of Abraham (the Akedah) often became the structure for an edifice of glowing faith.

Isaac was not sacrificed; but a million children died in the camps. The survivors of these events—all the survivors, all of the Western world—need new poetry and prayer after emerging out of the darkest circle of the Inferno. In the Jewish tradition, there are those who have turned to silence as an act of faith or in rejection of faith. The believers remind us of the Biblical tradition of Aaron who was silent after the death of his sons—the shortest, most anguished sentence in the Torah: "va-yi-dom Aharon—and Aaron was silent." Aaron's silence

7

was the silence of humility, a continuing, strong affirmation of God in a world which had become dark. We honor the silent mourners in our midst, the children of Aaron. Alongside of them, we see another company of silence. It is composed of those who have rejected the religious vision, who have lost the way to God and embrace the courage of despair. In a bleak and dark secular world, they speak for the majority. Yet that silence can lead to forgetting, can lead to ignorance. We need words. We need altars and rituals and worship. We know that the enormity of our loss cannot be placed into human discourse; the *tremendum* of the *shoah* is somewhere beyond the boundary of human understanding. But there comes a time, as it came to Job after his long and brooding silence, when one has to stand up and cry out. That cry is prayer. It addresses God, and it addresses humanity.

Elie Wiesel is the voice of the Jew in the Western world. When he speaks to the President in the White House, he is also the conscience of our society. When he teaches and publishes, when he lectures and dreams, he breaks the conspiracy of silence which has become the malady of our time:

> Watchman, what of the night? So many victims in so many places need help. We need, above all, to be shaken out of our indifference—the greatest source of danger in the world.
>
> For, remember: the opposite of love is not hate but indifference. The opposite of faith is not arrogance but indifference; the opposite of culture is not ignorance but indifference; the opposite of art is not ugliness but indifference. And the opposite of peace is indifference to both peace and war—indifference to hunger and persecution, to imprisonment and humiliation, indifference to torture and persecution.
> (Elie Wiesel, "Welcoming 1986," in *The Times*)

Indifference leads to silence. There must be words for those who care. Ignorance leads to silence. There must be records of past and present cruelties done in the world, so that each generation can remember—not only the evil of the past, but also the glowing goodness, the courage and the decency, which existed in the darkest days. In this text, Elie Wiesel brings us words to destroy indifference and to awaken remembrance. The words are small, glowing embers of despair. And hope. They are history. And they are prayers.

During the time of medieval persecutions, Jewish communities wrote "Memor-books," chronicles of what happened outside and inside the Jewish community when Death came uninvited and with violence. The books traveled to the outer limits of human existence, to days of destruction which matched the days of creation, of nights and days in which there were no hiding places. Jews fled here and there, toward each corner of the Holocaust Kingdom; and destruction found them. They died alone and unknown. Now it is time for memory to find them, for humanity to shake off its indifference, for prayer and ritual to place them into the heart of a caring world. Elie Wiesel has taken six pages out of the Memor-book of the Holocaust; and we have tried to fashion a chronicle for every home and place of prayer so that remembrance may awaken for six memorial candles against the backdrop of absolute night.

The stories in our text are ragged and torn, six pathways that lead to destruction. They are not beautiful tales. They speak of death in life and of life in death. But they are memorable. And they are true. Poetry becomes prayer, and fiction becomes fact. As we read them, we are drawn into an undefined landscape where "train people" pass unseen through villages and towns, where names and identities shift but stay the same—Havah becomes Bracha, Rachel searches for her children through the millennia, Baruch can be called Zelig or Yaakov—and where Death celebrates the climax of Creation and where the Kiddush becomes the Kaddish. In the text we find the chaos of that time, the incompleteness and un-certainty of those days when logic was foolishness, when plans were of no avail. Death came to the tutored and to the untaught, to the wise and to the foolish, to the wanderer upon the road and to the frightened child in the hiding place. The fool and the saint died. The old and the young. And a web of words is woven here so that we can remember them all, even when we cannot do justice to them. Six Yahrzeit candles to recite six mil-lion names? We do not have the strength. We do not have the time. We do not have the knowledge. That is why the six moments of human life are placed into the framework of Divine Creation, why the six days of Cre-ation, with its ever repeating pattern of night and day—"and it *was* night, and it *was* day"—becomes the frame-work for a text which is also liturgy.

Something frightening happened to this framework when the chronicler placed six events of the Holocaust into it. The framework broke apart. Behind the Six Days of Creation there appeared the Six Days of Destruction. Destruction is always part of Creation. It is the tool, is the material, the knowledge of decay in all that lives, the knowledge of the darkness which will not go away when there is light. Elie Wiesel ponders upon the completion of Creation on the Sixth Day: "va-y'chulu ha-shamayim: and the heavens collapsed, and the earth as well"—God stopped too soon, as it were; the original chaos and the power of Evil had not yet been removed; and the Kiddush becomes the Kaddish.

Can we take these six stories into our lives? The answer is already given. Once we have read the sto-ries, they will not leave us. They are part of human his-tory, and part of our own memories. That somber beat "And it came to pass in those days . . . it came to pass" has been the language of the chronicler and of the story teller, always arresting, always commanding. But we must do more with the text. It is to be taken into our lit-urgy, into all authentic liturgies which acknowledge hu-man suffering and cannot pray if this anguish is excised from the awareness of the individual at prayer, of the community at worship. This is a painful book. Pain can heal. If the pain is too deep, it can still purify.

We must remember this.

It is our prayer that you will take this book into your home, into your heart. It should be read again and again, as an act of remembrance which will place the dignity of pain and grief upon all those lives which cross the abyss between Creation and Destruction. And then these memories should enter the liturgies of all traditions, in many houses of worship. A community will sit together. It will pray, and it will weep. Jews light their own memorial candles as remembrancers. There is also a duty for Christians: the Holocaust is a deep and abiding problem to the devout and concerned believer of the Christian faith, and Christian liturgies have begun to reflect that awareness. Our partnership with the various communities of faith and concern brings this memorial into all situations where there are those who care, those who know that Destruction lurks beneath the surface of Creation. And it was evening . . . and it was morning . . . and it was evening. That was the beginning for a journey of discovery which took Adam and Eve through pain into light and then once more into pain. Their children have walked together on that path, and must not be separated. We share the pain of the Six Days of Destruction.

Little remains to be said. The basic text of this book is Elie Wiesel's chronicle: six stories to be read together, as one; to be read separately; to be read in private; to be read in public. To be remembered. The text is complemented by the illustrations of Mark Podwal, who has illustrated many of Eli Wiesel's works. Black fire and white fire come together here as another dimension of the Torah of Creation, of the destruction which has turned our world into a burnt-out, blackened star. A short meditation, a prayer, precedes each section to remind us of the complex pattern of remembrance which is at the heart of a memorial book. Not only the events, but also the continuity of the dialogue with God are part of any tale which begins with " . . . now it came to pass in those days . . . " Is it enough? As Elie Wiesel said in another text: only the story itself remains. And it *must* suffice.

"bereshit bara elohim et ha-shamayim v'et ha-aretz. V'ha-aretz
ha-y-ta tohu va-vohu, v'choshech . . . "

"in the beginning of God's creating the heaven and the earth,
there was chaos, and darkness . . . "

erev rosh hashanah 5748
approaching the year 5748
of creation.

London.

The Six Days of Destruction

the First day

In the beginning of God's creating the heaven and the earth, the earth was without form and void. And darkness hovered over the face of the deep. And the Spirit of God moved upon the face of the waters. And God said: let there be light: and there was light. And God saw the light, that it was good; and God divided the light from the darkness. And God called the light Day, and the darkness He called Night. And it was evening and it was morning: the first day. (Genesis 1:1–5)

Lord God of Creation: we thank You for the light and for the darkness, for the dark flame which engraved Your letters into the firmament of creation, for the unending light shining out of the Six Days of Creation. O Lord our God, help us to find that light again in the Days of Destruction. Your daughter Hava looks for it in vain. It was swept up as shards on the streets on a night of crystal, it was lost in the chambers of advocates who killed souls with stamps. There was no shining in the skylights of the cattle trains. It was dark there. Yet somewhere, underneath the shells pushed back and forth in cruel sport, the light is shining. Break the shells, O Lord; let the light come forth. And help us to remember those who moved from light to darkness. We praise You, Lord, Giver of light and darkness.

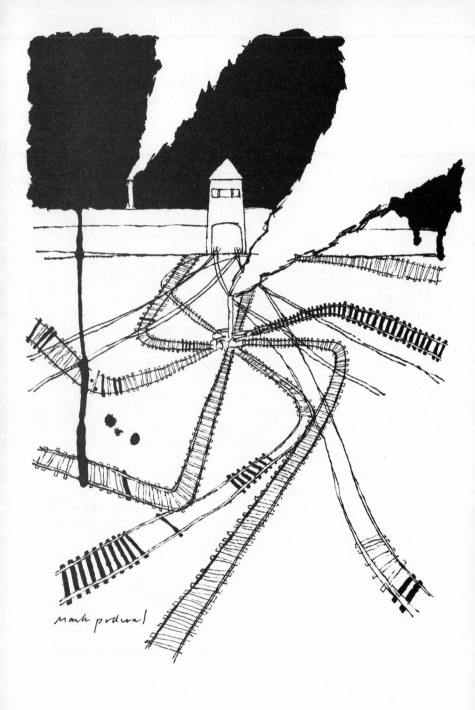

mark podwal

And it came to pass in those days that terror denied all languages and frontiers. It became a universe of its own. In those days, it imprisoned and mutilated its victims and their dreams, and then reduced them to ashes. It deprived human beings of the sun, the heart of happiness, and the soul of salvation. In those days, it ruled in the high and the low places. Its reign seemed eternal.

There was Hava, who wanted to escape. She was prepared to leave her home, her neighbors, and the familiar streets of her town—Kreinsdorf, somewhere in Germany.

"Let us leave," she begged her husband. "Let us leave, Baruch!"

"Not yet," he answered her.

They did not know, they could not know, that in the eyes of the enemy their fate was already sealed.

In those days, it was the enemy who held the Book of Life and Death open before him. It was he who inscribed therein the names in letters of black fire or in letters of white fire.

"What good is haste?" asked Baruch. "We have time. Our children go to school here. Our possessions tie us to the land. And our friends do not dream of running away. What right do we have to separate ourselves from our community?"

"I am afraid," said Hava. "That's all. I am afraid. That suffices."

"I am also afraid. So? We have been afraid for two thousand years. As long as a Jew is alive and as long as he is a Jew, he is filled with fear. Is that reason enough for him to leave everything and to rush into the unknown?"

Vayehi erev, vayehi voker . . .

And the days passed and so did the nights. Baruch was not only called Baruch; Hava had other names as well. Everywhere, the same anguished debate divided parents and children in Jewish homes. And none of them could possibly suspect that somewhere, in some office in Berlin, the argument had already been re-solved.

"For the love of our daughter who is expecting a baby, for the love of our son who intends to serve God, let us leave. Let us leave while it is still possible!" said Hava who elsewhere was also called Leah or Sheindl or Rose or Feigele.

"Where would you like to go?" answered Baruch, whose name was also Zelig or Yaakov or Leon. "We are known here. Anywhere else, we would just be un-wanted strangers."

They were both right; but they could not know this.

In those days, one had to be a pessimist to survive. One had to tear oneself away from one's habits, from the comforts of family love, from the intimate cruelties which bind a family together. In those days, one had to leave quickly, had to go as far away as possible, leave behind the possessions acquired by previous generations with the sweat of their brows and their tears.

In those days, one had to surrender to extreme despair. All illusions had to go which bound Jews to the present: "That's how it is, and we can't do a thing about it!" The Jew can only live by going beyond himself. He exists only in the past and in the future, never in the present if he is cut off from his past and his future. To survive, one had to turn one's back on the immediate and run until the breath gave out, until one found one-self naked on the other side of the frontier, on the other side of the abyss.

But a collective departure into exile is not a simple matter. A community does not voluntarily up-root itself overnight. The heavens must intervene. There must be a sign, a clear command, an unmistakable portent. The earth must tremble.

Unfortunately, Death came far too slowly. Baruch did not see its approach. Few had the courage to look Death in the face as it drew near to envelop thousands of Jewish communities which still flourished but were already marked to die.

"We shall live, we shall survive," said Baruch. "The ordeal is not new. We shall overcome it."

"But the threats?" asked Hava, seized with growing panic, "and the round-ups? And the burnt-out synagogues? And the concentration camps?"

"The enemy is barbaric and cruel, and the hate he stirs up is contagious, fertile and malignant. I know that," answered Baruch. "But his vociferous shouts need not be taken seriously. He will calm down. He must. After all, we are living in the twentieth century. Moreover, we live in a country whose cultural heritage and influence are the envy of other nations: it isn't here and it isn't now that they are going to massacre the Jews."

Meanwhile, the enemy imposed his laws. Jews were forbidden to hold official positions. To employ Gentiles. To possess anything other than their memories.

Decrees, persecution, brutality. Burned: sanctuaries, books, holy scrolls. Humiliated: old men, women upon whom they spat. Expelled: families, by the thousands, the thousands. An entire people—our people—was outlawed. They could beat us with impunity. They could put us into prison, steal our clothes, torment us and torture us without fear of punishment.

"We can still leave," said Bracha. "Let us go!"

"It is only a sickness from which the government is suffering," replied her husband, speaking for numerous husbands. "Our country is a great country. It will be able to exorcise these bloodthirsty demons."

"Our country?" said Bracha. "This is no longer our country. We are no longer German citizens. We are no longer citizens of any country."

Bracha, poor Bracha, was right, of course. Germany had disinherited its Jews. From Cologne to Frankfort, from Munich to Baden-Baden, the Jews knew themselves to be rejected, disowned, pilloried.

Nevertheless, they could still leave.

The day came when the gates were closed. The Jews in Germany were caught in the trap. Branded, isolated, doomed to solitude, to shame and to death. Crammed into sealed cattle trucks, they howled their despair into the night. The wind carried their lamentations to the four corners of the earth, but men and nations near and far refused to listen. Unwanted in Germany, detested in Poland, these stateless people, "train people," retraced the same route along the same border, never going far from any territory, sleeping where they did not eat, eating where they did not sleep. Condemned to wander by rail, they disembarked at a wretched and starving place, waiting for help which was slow in coming and for a miracle which was slow in happening.

It all came to pass in those days: the attempt on a life in Paris, the Night of the Broken Glass in Germany. Organized madness. Mass arrests. Unending queues at the consulates: the Jews had woken up at last and were ready to leave. Only now the civilized countries—the enlightened, hospitable countries—did not want them to come at all.

"Everyone is generous at our expense," read the German headlines. "Jews for sale and no buyers."

There were hypocritical conferences, insincere declarations, tears and words which hid the sickening, loathsome coldness of heart of the leaders of the so-called Free World.

"Where can we go?" wondered Baruch. "What country would agree to take us in? What government would give us a visa?" Everywhere, the answer was the same: later, impossible, come back, write, fill in these forms—and those, show proof that you are rich, or that you are poor, that you have relatives in France or in the United States, that you are not going to be a burden upon the society which may possibly take you in; we say advisedly: possibly.

Mr. Consul, Mr. Vice Consul: modern princes, jealous, envied and adored gods. A gesture, Mr. Consul!

A word, Mr. Vice Consul! Our life depends on your look, our happiness on your kindness . . . a visa was worth more than eternal truth, a rubber stamp more than divine promises . . .

But the heart of the world stayed cold and hard and dry, like a stone. The soul of humanity remained arid and complacent. The leaders proved to be inhuman in their refusal to hear the victims' cries for help . . .

Poor generation which tottered in the twilight before disappearing. Poor humanity which justified doubt and disgust. Wretched History where so many innocents drowned in blood and in flames . . .

"Where *can* we go?" Baruch asked himself. "I would go anywhere." Unhappily, in the accursed world, there was no place with that name. No one was interested in the Jews—except the executioner.

Then Hava took her pen and wrote a letter to God:

"Holy Creator of all worlds, take pity on thy children; show them a place where they can live in peace and serve thee. Every people has a land, every being a happy memory. We have nothing. Every family has a home, every mother craves for serenity: why are we deprived of these things? Thou hast placed us here on earth for a reason. I should like to know why. Is it possible the reason no longer exists? Thou who givest life, O Lord, is it thy will to see it vanish in the mist? I ask thee, O Lord God, King of the Universe, for I have no one else to speak to. Yes, I have a husband and we have children; they would understand me. But if I were to open my mouth, if I began to say all that I have in my heart, I would not be able to control myself. I would scream and scream so loudly that even the deaf would begin to hear."

She hid the letter in her prayer book. And when, with her family, she was taken to a ghetto far away in the East, she did not forget to take it with her. And so she was able to deliver it in person.

Vayehi erev, vayehi voker . . .

the Second day

And God said: Let there be a firmament in the midst of the waters, and let it divide the waters . . . and He called the firmament Heaven. And it was evening and it was morning: the second day. (Genesis 1:6–8)

Many waters cannot quench love, nor can floods drown it. In the ghetto, in the bunkers, Your people continued to love You . . . but the firmament called heaven was very far away . . . and it was not water which flooded the streets, red as the Nile . . .

Lord: after the Flood came the rainbow and its promise . . . after the night comes the morning . . . and the night. There are so many new stars on the firmament of Heaven now . . . blue stars from the ghettoes . . .

O God, Who created heaven and earth: when You join them together, let heaven prevail and not earth. Let the stars in their courses fight the madness of this time. May they shine in our prayers. May we remember them. Help us, O Lord, Who dividest the world: help us to make it whole.

It came to pass in those days that heaven and earth were reunited to destroy men and to cover them with shame. The people of creation were driven from creation. They were condemned to die for nothing, the very people sworn to sanctify life and the meaning of life.

"I do not understand," muttered a woman called Sarah. She was alone in her shelter. That astounded her. The evening before she had been surrounded by her family. Where had they gone? "I am going mad," said Sarah to herself.

She got up with difficulty. Her body hurt, her eyes hurt. It was night in the cellar. Yesterday evening, before going to sleep, I thanked the Lord for having spared us all . . . yesterday evening there was light here . . . someone has put it out . . .

Sarah listened. She listened with all her being. It was only a bad dream: my husband is asleep, our happiness is intact . . . Our three children are playing or telling each other scary stories . . . I dream that I am dreaming.

When did she start living under ground? "I no longer have a memory," thought Sarah, and felt her blood freezing in her veins. It was not that she no longer remembered things or events, but she had forgotten their sequence. In her mind, Sarah saw everything happening at the same time:

The day of her wedding coincides with that of the birth of her firstborn, which coincides with the day the Germans came; Rosh Hashanah falls on the same day as Tisha b'Av. Sarah and her family celebrate the Seder with songs and yet it is not Passover but Purim and the Jews are all assembled in the big square and an officer talks to them in a monotonous and murderous voice: he speaks and Death responds Amen.

It came to pass in those days . . . it came to pass on that day . . .

"You are all going to be evacuated," said the officer. "This town is going to be purged of its Jews. It is your fault. You wanted to be alone, separate. That, you shall have. Henceforth, you will live with your own kind. Henceforth, you will breathe the air of the ghetto," said the officer, and the dead of the past and the dead of the future responded Amen.

The ghetto and its yellow and black stars. The ghetto with its ghosts. Illusion and anguish. Let us rejoice, brethren! See us in the Jewish kingdom of our dreams. Jewish officials, Jewish authority, Jewish discipline, Jewish police, Jewish atmosphere. Derision from the pessimists: you are stupid and blind—you do not see that this kingdom is no more than a graveyard. As for Sarah, she thought of the future for her three children, of her husband's wisdom and of divine mercy. "God is not blind," she said. "Even if we are, He is not."

Just like time, space is malleable. Sarah perceived this from their first day in the ghetto. Four families occupied a miserable hovel. One crowded together a bit, and then a bit more, and then again: oh yes, it is bearable. "Here am I—I, who have always detested promiscuity," thought Sarah. "Now, one has to learn to swallow it. And to hold one's tongue. And to stare into space, just into space." One night her husband complained of pains in his chest. The doctor was willing to examine him, but outside: he could not manage to thread his way across the room.

And it came to pass in those days that life, nevertheless, continued. In spite of hunger and cold, in spite of manhunts, the children studied. Old men told their tales. The young people flirted and made plans: to escape, to get married, to have a career. Tell me, what do you think you will do after the war? When it's all over, tell me, where will you go? And each one answered in his own way. "How stupid we have become," thought Sarah. As if questions have answers in times of war!

In a time of ordeal, stupidity reigns. Intelligence has no part to play. Cunning, yes. Nothing else. I mean, nothing else apart from might. And money. It was easy to see this in the ghetto. The rich got richer, the people with power had other thoughts from us, their subjects . . . as though the enemy had adopted separate, opposing plans of actions for different types of Jews!

"What about me?" thought Sarah. "Me—who never had either power or money. How have I managed to survive alone in this shelter, alone in the dark, against this night? To whom do I owe this good or bad luck? Who has interceded for me on high?"

A prayer formed on her lips, the one she recites at the end of Shabbat: "God of Abraham, Isaac and Jacob, watch over us." But it was not Shabbat today. What day was it, what night? When would day break? Sarah thought about her loved ones. A united, happy family; with a flourishing business, excellent friends, and a feeling of security. Romtche, the husband: gentle, kind and thoughtful. On their wedding day, after the ceremony, he had said to her: "We are going to make a home, a Jewish home. Promise me one thing."

"What?"

"In our house beggars will feel at ease. God loves them. Let us love them too."

Now it is we who are the beggars. Does God love us?

Sarah thought about her three children. Two boys and a girl. Berenyou, the oldest, was shy. Srolenyou, the youngest, was not. He was wild, daring, full of charm. Between them came Perele, called after her great-grandmother, Perele the Pious, of whom it was said that she had secret powers. The ghetto had changed all three. Berenyou, always active and alert, brought back food; Srolenyou spent his nights reciting Psalms; Perele, twelve years old, was active in a Zionist youth movement. Only Romtche had stayed the same. He was never impatient. He lived in expectation.

"I have faith in God," he said. "If God wants to see us suffer, it is because we deserve it. It is for our good. Every time someone suffers it brings the coming of the Messiah nearer. We suffer so much: we must be very close to the time. I feel it."

Lately, Romtche thought only of the Messiah. He talked about him endlessly. He murmured his name while wandering through the streets, while saying his prayers morning and evening, while giving lessons to young and old in secret classrooms. He delved into every sentence, even the mildest, most simple phrase, to discover a sign: "In the beginning God created the heavens and the earth," says the Torah. The letters of the first word contain several expressions: *esh*—fire; *rosh*—head; *osher*—happiness; *shir*—song. The First Man will be called upon to bring us the song of ultimate happiness out of the fire.

"But where does the Messiah come into it?" they asked him.

He answered gently: "His name precedes Creation. The Messiah predates Bereshit; he is part of the Ineffable . . . "

Poor, poor Romtche. People shook their heads when they saw him. He is losing his mind, they said. Sarah protected him, defended him. Mad? Her husband? Why mad? Because he believes in God? Because he wants to hasten Redemption? But then, good people, his madness is better than your sanity!

In those days, there was a madman in the ghetto, a real madman whom they called "Milou the Fool." In Romtche, Milou saw a companion, a brother in arms.

"Romtche," he would shout, "people are stupid! Take no notice of what they are saying. They are just jealous of you and of me, jealous of our po-si-tion, you know? From where we are, we can see a long way! We see the Messiah, and he sees us too! Mad? Us? Then he is mad as well! A mad Messiah, ha, ha, ha!"

In truth, everyone was going mad. Nature itself seemed to have set aside its immutable laws. Sometimes after an "Aktion," people hid at night and went out during the day. Bonds were formed in an instant and would last a lifetime: except that life was gone in a twinkling. Dwellings became empty ten times a week and yet the ghetto always seemed crowded and full so that you could scarcely breathe. Families were separated, others were formed, and nobody understood a thing.

"It is clear," said Romtche; "we are living in messianic times."

"He is mad," cried Milou the Fool. "Bravo, brother!"

Meanwhile, on the edge of despair, the ghetto had sudden bursts of enthusiasm, even ecstasy. Killers tracked down children to annihilate them. Yet in the ghetto children went to school, studied the Bible, chanted the Talmud. The sick received care and love, while—a day or a week or a month later—they would be buried alive.

"Bravo!" cried Milou.

"Amen," said Romtche.

And it came to pass . . . that one evening . . . Perele came home with bad news. Her youth movement had reliable contacts on the outside. They claimed that the Germans were preparing to liquidate the ghetto. Permanently. The Jews had a choice: run away; hide; or fight. Run away? Quicker said than done. For that one needed friends, support, places to shelter and very, very much money. Fight? Romtche and Sarah were not made to fight with guns in their hands. There was only one choice left: discover a shelter, a bunker. How? Don't laugh: it was Milou, Milou the Fool, who knew how to arrange it. He went to see a big dealer and persuaded him to take him in, together with his friends.

"It will mean bad luck for you if you refuse," he threatened. "The Messiah will come and you will not be here to welcome him."

The bunker: spacious, airy, quite pleasant. Sarah lived through hours of intense happiness there. Impossible? You have never known anguish, then. In the distance, the sound of the killers: dogs barking, guns firing, grenades exploding. This way! Come out, stinking Jews! Over here! They are getting nearer. They are in our street. In the block opposite. Next door. Careful! Quiet! They are here! They are walking overhead!

No one breathed. No one dared look or think in case a look or a thought could make a noise. Death. You do not know what Death is like. It hears what is not even said aloud, it sees all that wants to stay unseen. Death has a thousand eyes. It is hard to deceive, hard to avoid. Death scents life, sniffs it out, draws it up and inhales it the better to snuff it out. Oh, see it go. Death has gone away. You want to shout, to scream for joy. Too soon. Death might come back. Be quiet, you who live! Play dead if you value your life!

For five days and five nights the inhabitants of the bunker played dead. The Germans were installed in the apartment above. Sarah could hear them laughing, drinking, snoring. Immobility lay heavy upon them and crushed them: infinite torture. The dealer took the first opportunity to go out for air. He returned an hour later. Someone caught sight of him and denounced him.

"Jews out!" No one moved. Shots. Violent explosions. "I am wounded," someone cried. "I am blind," answered someone else. "It is the Messiah!" shouted Milou the Fool. The bunker was shaken by a new explosion and Sarah felt herself penetrated by a shattering light which made her lose consciousness.

Is it a madman? The Messiah? Sarah felt someone sharing her solitude. She wanted to get away somewhere, anywhere, but she lacked the strength. She felt the ghetto weighing down on her. It was the dead who shared her solitude; the ghetto was their communal cemetery.

Vayehi erev, vayehi voker. The day is ending. As it fades, it makes such a great and shocking noise that it scatters the madness from one corner of the world to the other. And it goes beyond, far beyond.

the Third day

And God said: let the waters under the heaven be gathered together in one place and let the dry land appear . . . the Earth. And the waters He called the Sea. And it was good. And God said: Let the earth create . . . and the earth brought forth grass, and herb yielding seed . . . and trees yielding fruit, fruit giving seed . . . and it was good. And it was evening and it was morning: the third day. (Genesis 1:9–13)

And we rejoiced in Your gifts, O Lord: earth giving life, feeding all creatures—until the Destruction came. The trees of the forest turned away when the death columns marched to their graves. The grass tried to hide the killings. The fruit trees did not want to feed the murderers. Earth knew it was next on the list: poisoned rivers and polluted air, a dusty sky filled with the ashes of believers . . . O Lord: will water and land be good again? Will they help us to remember? And what will the land remember when it is called Babi Yar? What will the hanging tree remember? Create anew, O Lord: spread over us new tabernacles of Your peace.

And this is the story of a ghetto. No, of a family in the ghetto. No, of a member of that family. No, this is just the story of a candle. It is the same story.

It came to pass in those days, once upon that time, that there was a wise and pious man called Old Itzikl. In truth, the nickname suited him: he seemed old. It was said of him that he was born old. But his wife was young. And radiant in her beauty. She was called Miriam but everyone knew her as Mirele. They had six children. The oldest, Baruch, was fifteen; the youngest, Srulik, three. They were a happy family, serene and welcoming. Itzikl studied, Mirele ran the business, and the children occupied themselves as best they could; at Cheder, in the neighbor's garden, in the market or with the wandering beggars whose very bearing suggested mysterious and forbidden things.

Then the war broke out. Poland surrendered. The Jews asked each other what the future had in store for them. "Oh, I live in hope," said Itzikl, and he explained why. "Times may change, but God never changes." Mirele was of the same opinion; and so were the children. How could it be otherwise? Ever since the world began, Jews had suffered; ever since there had been a strong and wicked enemy, Jews had waited for the Redemption.

Yet it came to pass in those days that the enemy became more and more ferocious, more and more powerful. Like others in occupied Poland, the Jews in Itzikl's town were expelled from their homes. They now had to learn how to exist in the shadow of the barbed wire.

"I live in hope," said Old Itzikl. And since the children waited for more, he added: "I promise you that all will end well. God alone shapes our end. Trust in God."

In those days, the trust was put to the test innumerable times. Day by day it was worse. Imagine: the chief rabbi of the town forced by German officers to clean the pavement, to sweep it with his beard. And all around, proud soldiers, warriors puffed up with their victories, slapped their thighs in merriment. Imagine: a distinguished officer, a man of good family, orders Jewish children to run, like rabbits, and then he takes out his revolver and begins shooting at the terrified living targets, scattering them, mowing them down. Imagine: no, let us not imagine anymore. In those days, the executioners had more imagination than their victims. The victims were always taken by surprise. It was impossible to predict the next blow, the next measure. What could you do? The executioners were too clever; they did their job to perfection. They knew how to demobilize the ghetto, to disarm it, to neutralize it. More precisely, they knew how to trap it, fool it, deceive it—to blind it.

They used every science and every technique. Among them were philosophers and psychologists, doctors and artists, experts in management and specialists in poisoning the mind: all collaborated in this patriotic national mission which consisted of sowing death among the children and their parents.

Old Itzikl, always an optimist, refused to believe the rumors which had recently started circulating. Summary executions out there, on the far side of the forest. Deportees leaving in sealed railway trucks. "God will remember," said Itzikl, "and He will see to everything."

One day he seemed shaken. Shocked. He had been attending a secret meeting at the house of one of the Hassidic rabbis in the ghetto. A ghost had returned from out there, a traveler returning from another world, who told what had happened to him and what he had seen.

"There were a hundred of us leaving the ghetto. We crossed the wall. It was a lovely day. Mild. We were moving slowly toward the forest. All was silent. Then, suddenly . . ."

He broke off, too overcome to continue. Someone gave him a glass of water. He was sweating and had difficulty in breathing. They begged him to go on. To tell all. And he did. In short, jerky sentences. The names of the old people. The terror of the children. The wild, prolonged cries of the mothers. You know Zelig the shoemaker and Tevye the butcher? Promoted to gravediggers. At the head of a team of young people they dug four graves. The children watched wide-eyed, without understanding. The adults, stupefied, did not budge. An old grandmother murmured a prayer, a Hasid smiled to himself. As for the soldiers, they looked bored. And it was still a lovely day. And mild.

"And I . . . " said the ghost. He stopped again, incapable of going on. "And I . . . " His shoulders moved in a shrug. Weariness? Despair? Madness? His lips remained half open. "And I . . . I saw everything. I heard everything. Gathered it all together. Brought it all back. All their lives are in mine. Their deaths, too . . . "

The people shook their heads and rubbed their eyes in disbelief. "He is mad," one of them said. "He is hungry," said another. They were wrong. He was neither hungry nor thirsty; he was no more mad than you or I. Only more lonely.

"What do you think, Itzikl?" asked his wife Mirele. "Do you think it is possible he was telling the truth, that human beings could commit such crimes?"

Old Itzikl did not answer immediately. He waited until his six children were there. And some neighbors from the slums next door. Then, his gentle gaze wandering over his family and his friends, Old Itzikl began to speak.

"God commands us to live in wait for His messenger and redeemer. Waiting is easy when things go well. It is when nothing goes right that we must wait! When everything seems lost forever, when humanity has lost the reason for its existence and society has shed its masks and pretexts—it is then that we Jews must sanctify our hope and proclaim it in the sight of the world!"

He seemed different, Itzikl. Less old, perhaps. More excited and animated than ever. Did he realize that his audience was moved but skeptical? No one said anything, but he must have sensed it. Suddenly he got up, went over to a corner, opened his talit bag and took out a long white candle. He displayed it with pride.

"Look," he said. "I have kept this candle to light in His honor and to illumine the way. I promise you: we shall see it shine one day . . . "

It was very strange, but this time the people were with him. The candle became a rare and precious object belonging to another world, to another time. As long as the candle was there, nothing would happen to them.

"Let me tell you the story of this candle," said Old Itzikl. "It was given to me by my teacher, the Tzaddik of Gorobetz, of blessed memory. He said to me: 'Keep it for a special occasion!' I thought—for my wedding. Then—for that of my oldest son. Now I know. This candle deserves an even more important occasion. And you will see: we shall all take part in it . . . "

Some of the neighbors were taken away the following day; they did not have the required work cards. A month later, the whole street was evacuated. Itzikl and Mirele, with their six hungry and exhausted children, merged with the mass of people pushed toward the gates of the ghetto by the soldiers. It was autumn now. A cool wind blew through the trees and made them sing. The sky, a blue screen, clouds, lost in the heights. Farm noises in the distance. Voices of plowmen.

"The ghost was telling the truth," said Mirele quietly. Itzikl did not reply. He looked ahead. There, there was the end of the forest. He knew what would happen. They would get some of the young men to dig graves. But he was wrong. The graves were dug, ready to receive the children. A rabbi recited the Viddui. A porter rebuked him:

"Do not tell lies, Rabbi. Do not say we have sinned. You know that we have not sinned. Do not say we have acted falsely. We have not been false to God or to His Law."

The rabbi seemed to agree but continued to chant in a very low voice, full of pain. "Father," asked a child, "what prayer should we say?"

Itzikl, silent all this time, murmured the Shema as if to himself: Hear, O Israel, the Lord is our God, the Lord is One. "I know that," said the child. After a moment's silence, it added: "Thank you, father."

Soon it will be Death who supplies all the responses. It is Death who will issue all the orders. And it will all seem natural. As if it were part of a design as old as the world. What good would it do to rebel? One does not rebel against the laws of creation. What good would it do to weep? The world is not worth it. And heaven? Heaven is far away.

It is on earth that it is going to happen, it is on earth that it is happening. Men removed their clothes; women too. Whoever refused was beaten. The others were slaughtered. Itzikl was one of the last. "And I . . ." he said, without completing his thought. "And I what? I who? And I . . ."

Suddenly, Old Itzikl remembered something important. He opened the bag where he kept his tallit and tephilin, rummaged around in the bottom and brought out a candle. He tried to light it but did not succeed. He renewed his efforts, concentrating so hard he looked like a madman. Did he see his first child fall into the pit? His second? The last one? I do not know what he saw. I only know what he did: he finally succeeded in lighting his precious candle. And he lifted it high above his head. At that precise moment the life of his last child was extinguished . . .

Vayehi erev, vayehi voker . . .

the Fourth day

And God said: Let there be lights in the firmament of the heaven to divide the day from the night; and let them be for signs, and for seasons, and for days, and years . . . two great lights; the greater light to rule the day . . . the lesser the night; and he made the stars . . . and it was good. And it was evening and it was morning, the fourth day. (Genesis 1:14–19)

O Lord Who made sun and moon and stars: we thank You for these gifts which sustain us. How could we approach the Sabbath without waiting for the stars? How meet the day without the strong sun rejoicing as it runs its course? How could we bless the New Moon? But Lord: what happened to the days and nights of destruction when there was no division? There was only darkness in the sealed railway cars. No sun or moon or stars to help Rachel find her children, to help her weep for them. She wept in darkness. Those tears are precious to us, stars in a different nightscape, diadems in her crown. We thank you for Rachel. But let the sun and moon and stars rise up again to divide light and darkness. And we will praise You.

A train in the night. A whistle in the night. Not daring to breathe, her nerves stretched painfully, Rachel listened. The carriage seemed peaceful, at rest. The transport was asleep or, like her, it pretended to sleep. Where are we going? Through the small skylight, a scrap of sky: a symbolic sign? We are going up to heaven, Rachel said to herself.

She looked around for her family, squatting on the floor there beside her. She did not see them. But she felt them, she sensed them. Yekel, her husband, was sleeping with his head on his knees. Leah, the oldest, was dreaming with her mouth open. Shimon, the little one, would soon cry that he is hungry. Her parents, like true grandparents, looked after the little ones. This is the first time I have traveled with my parents since I married, thought Rachel. Where are we going now? I do not ask for salvation, Lord, I only ask You to let me know.

In those days, no one knew. Yet someone in that carriage should have known. The rabbi of the community. The president of the community. The various go-betweens who had connections and contacts on the outside. They were all present. A whole community of Israel was in that railway carriage. Another community was in the one in front of them. And a third in the one behind. The entire Jewish people were heaped up in cattle trucks, traveling somewhere. What if we were going to a wedding? Rachel asked herself, suddenly frightened by the lunacy of her question.

The journey had already lasted three days. But the family, the community, had expected it for two years. Sooner or later the ghetto would be liquidated and its inhabitants deported: one had known that from the beginning.

The problem was that all had refused to know it. Illusions had been preferable: The Germans would not dare. The authorities would not allow it. The others need us. We are their doctors, their pharmacists, their scholars, their protectors, their colleagues. Imagine a Jewish town in Poland, Lithuania, Hungary or the

Ukraine without Jews!

The killers and their specialists allowed their prey to slide into uncertainty. From time to time a street, a group or a district received orders to get ready to leave. Simultaneously, the others were given reassurances: *You* have nothing to fear. *You* are going to stay with us, for us.

They hanged Shmulik to set an example: he had been in contact with the partisans in the forest. Meaning: he who is not in touch with the partisans may sleep easily in his bed. Then *they* killed Schreiber, the young secretary of the community, for having kept a diary. He had tried to explain: "It is my duty, for the sake of future generations . . . " They had burst out laughing. "In that case," they said, "we do not need you anymore." Moral: you must not write. He who abstains from writing, from interfering in other people's business, from looking toward the forest, from dreaming of future generations, has nothing to fear.

And the ghetto, diminished and mutilated, let itself be lulled by hope. The more *they* proved to be cruel, the more the survivors of each day responded with faith.

And now? No more ghetto, no more illusions, no more hope. There was nothing left. Only this wagon, asleep. Only this train roaring into darkness. And the whistle which tore the night apart, the night in us, the night we bear and which bears us like a curse.

The day before . . . or was it the day before that . . . Simhe the merchant had had an idea. He had managed to get hold of a pencil from someone, some pieces of paper from someone else, and he had begun to scribble messages that Leib Marshalik had thrown through the skylight. "You passers-by, look at these sealed wagons and remember: we are the last Jews of Ganarek. You who read these cries for help, do not pray for our souls; pray for your own."

The widow Tzirele went one better. *They* had killed her husband, Berl the musician, when she was eight months pregnant. Crying, she had put her child to the breast. Weeping, she rocked him. Sobbing, she had caressed him. Holding back her tears, she had taken her child and made him into a little parcel, carefully wrapped and tied. When the train slowed down, she had let the parcel slip down the side of the coach and drop out. Afterward, she had not stopped smiling. Women had spoken to her gently, but she did not reply. She only smiled.

"She is smiling because she is free," Rachel had thought. "She has no one left in the world. Now she can die. But I stay afraid."

In truth, everyone had been afraid. The whole convoy was dumb with fear. No one slept. With heavy hearts, men and women silently questioned the meaning of their lives: why so many trials, so many adventures, so many exiles, so many discoveries, if it was all to end in *this?*

This—what was it? Thirst. Hunger. Terror. Beyond that, dirt; exhaustion. By the third day of the journey, the Jews were assailed by a new feeling of weariness. Suddenly, they were not even curious anymore. Come what may, they no longer had the strength to try to read the signs. In the beginning, they had kept the old traditions. As far as possible, they had respected other people's rights to privacy. Natural functions were performed behind an improvised curtain. Water was shared out without argument. People had tried not to disturb their neighbors. Even the children had spoken more quietly. Now, since this morning, discipline had relaxed. The human machine was worn out. Their nerves had given way.

Where are we? Somewhere in Poland. Nothing more definite? Never mind. What is there to see through the skylight? Sky, clouds, stars, childhood memories, Sabbath prayers, chants, old pictures from another place . . . why look if it drives you mad? "I am afraid to look," Rachel said to herself. "I am afraid I will catch a glimpse of the future."

A cry in the night. A shiver went through the

convoy. A warning came to them mysteriously: Tomorrow, the world will not be the same. Tomorrow, the train will return empty. For you, there is no tomorrow.

"Who called out?" asked Rachel in a low voice, too low to be heard. But her question was taken up by dozens and dozens of voices. "Who, who, who called out?" Perhaps a madman. An invalid, no doubt. A dying man? Rachel also felt the need to shout. She controlled herself. "If I call out, everyone will start to shriek. There will be panic. It would be terrible. Above all, we must not upset the children."

Thousands of memories flooded her mind. First: her wedding. The singing, the dancing, the joy. The meal for the beggars. The blessings. She had been struck by a blessing given by a poorly-dressed man whom she did not know: "May you never leave your home." False blessing! We have all left our homes. Will we ever return? Other memories jostle, push, come to mind. A walk in the mountain with her husband. Rachel remembered the serenity of that day. Not a word was exchanged. Yet she was more aware of the presence of her husband than ever before or ever since. The birth of the children. The noise and excitement in the house. Parents, cousins, visitors with radiant faces. And the unknown poor man with the same blessing: "What do I wish you? May you never leave your home." A song started up in her memory, one heard long ago in her father's house. The words were sad, the melody was melancholy, heartbreaking: "*Kol b'Zion nishma,* a voice is heard in Zion, *v'Rachel m'vaka al baneha* and Rachel weeps for her children." Poor Rachel, who died journeying in a foreign land. Since then, so our tradition goes, she remains in the same place, at the crossroads of Jewish suffering, watching over Jewish children who have to leave their homes, accompanying them with her prayers.

"Who called out?" Again, bodies arose. "Rachel," she said. No. She had said nothing aloud. She had only thought it. It was not a reply but a wish, a desire. "Since you watch over us, Rachel, say something.

Give us something, if only a cry in the night."

Then, in that time and in those days, the train stopped suddenly. After a moment's hesitation, they tottered to their feet. It was the same in all the wagons. Those near the skylight described what they saw: a sea of light. Light bulbs by the thousands. And also: huge gigantic flames leaping out of factory chimneys to pierce the sky. "It looks like an important factory," someone said. "I wonder what they make here," said another.

Jews from Hungary and Poland, Czechoslovakia and Germany, Lithuania and France, Belgium and Holland, Norway, Esthonia and Austria: all had reached their destination. For the majority it was the end of their exile. For most of them, it was the end. The end of the world. The end of the story.

Vayehi erev, vayehi voker . . .

And there was darkness and there was light, a light filled with darkness. A cry tore through the silence: no one asked who had called out. They knew: it was Death. It was Death who had uttered the first cry.

It was the cry of victory.

Vayehi erev . . .

the Fifth day

And the Lord said: Let the waters bring forth living creatures . . . and fowl to fly above the earth . . . and He created great whales . . . and blessed the living: be fruitful and multiply, fill the waters, fill the land . . . and it was good . . . And it was evening and it was morning, the fifth day. (Genesis 1:20–23)

O Lord: You have created whales and wars. In deepest waters and high above, You have fashioned life which multiplies and moves to fulfill a portion of your plan. But in the night of destruction, Lord, birds refused to fly over the camps. Children no longer saw a butterfly. But some took part in the struggle for life in strange ways: one gun against a thousand, one moment of life in order to die—be fruitful and multiply, in order to replenish the soil. The day of creation taught reverence for life. Help us, O Lord, to find that road again. We search, we yearn for peace even as we recall the young lions who went out to war. Help us, O Lord.

When these events are known, they will become part of the eternal legend of the people Israel. Thanks to them, we will return to the source of our memory filled with sadness and pain, but also with fidelity and pride.

For it came to pass in those days: In a ghetto in the East, a dozen young Jews were gathered in a secret meeting place lit by a dirty, dust-covered light bulb. Tense and excited, they listened, sometimes incredulously, to their leader Yehuda, who told them of the battle to come.

"Our families are dead," Yehuda said hoarsely. "Our teachers are dead. Our friends are dead. We will soon be the last members of the community, the last Jews alive in this land. Then it will be our turn. Be prepared: our honor is at stake."

They were very young fighters. Yehuda, the oldest, was twenty. The others were younger. Teenagers with the eyes and gestures of old men. Among them were workers, Yeshiva students, a carpenter, a schoolboy.

"We are going to fight," said Yehuda. "The enemy only recognizes force. We will meet his force with ours."

His comrades accepted the argument. Yehuda was right: the enemy hates our physical weakness. They kill the sick. They detest our spiritual power. They mock our intellectuals. Only the strong, the workers, have the right to live, say the enemies. Fine. We will be strong, well trained and well equipped. And will we win? Of course not; we cannot win. Yehuda and his group were well aware of this. How could they defeat the strongest army in Europe? There comes a time when logic must be discarded, when you have to fight logic.

"Action," said Yehuda. "That will be our watchword. We are going to arm ourselves and resist."

"With what?" asked a timid voice.

"With . . . this!" said Yehuda. And he brought "this" out of his pocket: a revolver. Someone stepped back in terror. He had never seen a revolver except in the hands of killers.

"It cost its weight in gold," said Yehuda.

The training period began: how to hold the weapon, at what height, with a finger on the trigger. Keep calm; it is important to keep calm. Do not panic, do not get impatient, do not move until the target is clearly in your sights. And then . . .

One of them, Yerachmiel, was clumsy and ashamed of it. It was not his fault. He had never handled any weapon but the Torah. In hiding, he still studied the Talmud. Seeing his lips move in silent prayer, one understood that Yerachmiel was not made to use revolvers.

"Yehuda," he said. "Do you intend to defeat the German army with this revolver?"

"We will have more," said Yehuda.

"How many? Ten? Twenty? A hundred?"

Yehuda was silent for a long moment. That very night, or the night before, or the one after, that same discussion was going on in Bialystock and Vilna, Warsaw and Lublin, wherever the Jews were oppressed, persecuted, and decimated by the enemy.

The resistance movements in occupied Europe all received aid or encouragement—except for the Jews who did not receive help from the Free World. The others were sent messengers and instructors, money and weapons, radio equipment and materials for sabotage; their safety was a matter of concern. Links were maintained with those units; each one was supported. Why, Lord, did they discriminate against the *Jewish* fighters? Why were they doomed to oblivion, even contempt?

Here and there, warm-hearted men and women of good will had certainly taken up the Jewish cause. Some risked their lives to protect and feed them and to warn them of the dangers that lay ahead. But they were few . . . few and rare.

The Jews simply could not rely on much support from the so-called Aryan world. When a Jew managed to escape from the train that took him to Treblinka or Sobidor, few doors were opened to take him in and bind up his wounds. Sooner or later, he retraced his steps and rejoined the ghetto. It was the only place where people accepted him without mistrust.

But it came to pass in those days that everywhere within that closed universe of barbed wire, Jews without military experience were turning themselves into fighters. Boys and girls showed a courage and initiative which would have been envied by storybook heroes. The young women who carried hidden ammunition and coded messages; the young fighters who visited besieged communities, urging them to fight; the commanders who even without weapons managed to transform every building into a fortress and every person into a prince of warriors, bold and unyielding: where had they acquired so much knowledge, so much passion, so much determination to believe in themselves? They saw themselves able to change the flow of events, of changing the course of history! Let us not forget, brothers—let us never forget—that the first civilian uprising against Nazi Germany and its armies was not in the city of Warsaw but in the Warsaw Ghetto. A few hundred young Jews succeeded in holding off tanks, heavy artillery and flame throwers—and air force bombers. Day after day, week after week, the blazing ghetto resisted the attack, while outside, in the Aryan districts, people walked about arm in arm and found the spring sunshine pleasant and the spectacle entertaining! Think about it. Repeat it again and again.

The Jews were alone against the Germans. Alone against collaborators. Alone against those who had denounced them. Alone against neutral, passive, indifferent people. The fighters were alone, and their solitude was that of God. Yet they went on fighting. And forced the enemy to retreat. And showed the whole world that the SS were only mortal; and cowards.

The Jewish fighters were equal to their task because they were prepared. They were ready to confront their fate, to follow in the footsteps of their forefathers who had gathered around their spiritual teachers and declared themselves ready during the Crusades . . . during the pogroms . . .

But beware, my friends. Beware, brothers. Don't be carried away by affection and admiration for the fighters, don't make facile distinctions. Don't divide them into resistance fighters and weaklings. Even the heroes perished as victims; even the victims were heroes. For it came to pass in those days and in those places that a prayer on the lips was equal to a weapon in the hand. The mother who refused to abandon her children had as much worth as the fighter who led his men into battle. The sage consoled the condemned; the beggar gave his blessing; the teacher taught his disciples how to lead a holy life by risking his own: each resisted the Nazis in a special way. They all gave us examples to follow, messages to pass on to others. We are at one with them. We will always see ourselves in all of them.

Mordecai and Antek. Marek and Shimon. Abraham. All the names from all our books are on the Roll of Honor of the ghetto uprisings.

"Be prepared," said Yehuda. "Our heritage is at stake. What will they think of us, those ancestors of ours who went to their deaths to glorify the Name of God? What will future generations think of us when they try to understand the mystery of our disappearance?" Vayehi erev, vayehi voker . . .

And there were words, and there was silence. The movements of the dying were followed by other movements, those of the witnesses. And there was life, and there was death.

"Our dignity is at stake," said Yehuda.

Finally, someone dared to contradict him.

"No, Yehuda. It is wrong to claim that fighting is the only source of dignity. The Hasid who looks the murderer straight in the eye dies with dignity. The rabbi who chants his prayers as he goes toward the mass grave and the mystic who wraps himself in his tallit as he walks to Treblinka: do not tell me that they lack dignity."

Yehuda lost his self-assurance. "I did not say that. But, for the time being . . . "

The opponent remained obstinate: "We are not talking about Now, Yehuda. If we are going to fight, it is not for Now, but for Forever, for the eternity of our people. Otherwise, it would have no meaning!"

Yehuda smiled. "You speak of eternity? Here? Now?"

"Yes," replied the fighter. "Here and Now. It is eternity which gives significance to this moment. It is history which gives this moment its profound quality, which gives it richness as well as unhappiness. I chose to fight because I think of Abraham and Moses, of Rabbi Akiva and the Besht, of the scholars and their disciples throughout the centuries! For them? Yes. But not only for them. With them. It is with them as well that we shall go into battle . . . "

This is what came to pass in that ghetto in the East; this is the argument which took place when the young commander showed them all his revolver. In time, he bought more. The movement spread. It spread so much that when the attack came they put up a glorious resistance, even though it was not effective. All of them died in combat. When the tale comes to be told it will possess the exultant but sad intensity of an ancient legend of the people of Israel.

Vayehi erev, vayehi voker . . .

the Sixth day

And God said: Let the earth bring forth living creatures, each of their kind, cattle and creeping things, beasts of the earth . . . and it was good. And God said: Let us make man in our image, after our likeness, and let him have dominion over all . . . in God's image, male and female created He them. And God blessed them . . . and God saw everything that He had made, and behold, it was very good. And it was evening and it was morning, the sixth day. (Genesis 1:24–31)

Creator of humanity: You have blessed all of us, and You have given us dominion. Fashioned in Your image, we have ascended the high places of the world. We have explored the depths. We have come to know Your other children, our neighbors. Then came the Destruction. O Lord, how we have fallen. In the night of Sobibor, Treblinka, Birkenau, we have forgotten Your blessing. We have lost our identity; but we have been cursed with memories. O Lord, what will happen to us and to the world when the days of destruction are finished? Will the Kiddush of rest become the final kaddish? Will this world end? Will a new world begin? We do not demand answers, God. But if this is the last page of the human chronicles, assure us that we had the right to ask. And we will always glorify Your name: *yitgadal v'yitkadash sh'mey rabba . . .*

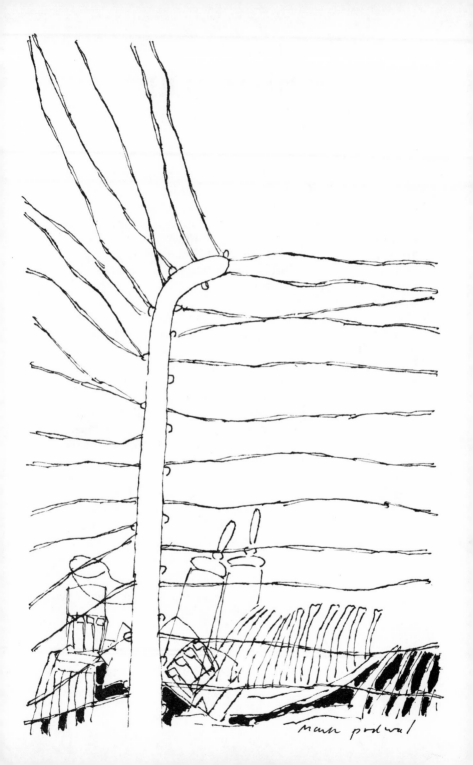

mark podwal

And there was light and there was darkness—total, absolute, enveloping, stifling darkness: the darkness of Final Breakdown. The darkness of the Great Separation.

Vayehi erev, vayehi voker, vayehi erev: flocks of people who had intermingled and had been joined together by links forged through the millennia were to be torn apart and sundered. Links re-form; but the flock will be sadly reduced, orphaned, and in mourning.

Birkenau, Treblinka, Sobibor: the processions came from all over, accompanied by shouting, howling, barking. They stopped for the moment of decision: Selektion, in front of a group of German officers who sometimes asked a few questions and then uttered one short phrase—"To the right"; "To the left." It was total and irrevocable separation. It was the difference between night and darkness, between the living and the dead, time and duration, hope and despair. One moment later, and everything had changed: the victims were already in another universe with its own laws and its own time.

Two words marked the frontier: too late. Too late to go back. Too late to feel regret or remorse. The victims no longer had the power to start again, to be different, to change direction. After the "ramp" they could only live or die—live *and* die—locked in a nightmare seven times accursed, seven times sealed.

Jan and Yohanan, Leah and Leanka, Irena and Susi, Baruch and Benedict and Benedekt, Avrohom and Albert, Rachel and Ibolya and Ginette and Dina: all the names of Jewish history, evoking picturesque and tormented countries and landscapes—all were to be dissolved here in ashes and oblivion.

Some were to die. Others—luckier? less lucky?—suffered and lost their identity. As some were deprived of their identity, so others were deprived of their death. Everything happened in a rush, quicker and quicker. The rhythm made dizzy, took away the breath. In a twinkling, families and clans and communities were broken up. Men on one side, women on the other. Children here, adolescents there. "I want to go with my mother," said a pretty blonde little girl. The kindly officer sent her after her mother. Her brother saw them together, hand in hand. He wanted to run after them, kiss them, say something to them—anything. But the crush of people had already borne them away, too far away; he could only try to follow them with his gaze.

"Come," said an old man to his terrified grandson. "Let us walk together. Give me your arm and try above all not to be afraid." Together they walked in the silent throng. Together they went forward toward a darker place under a flaming sky. Together they mounted the altar of their murdered love.

A few steps away, the living were engulfed in an abyss of misery and torture. The humiliation was organized, was practiced and worked out scientifically. Their clothing was removed, their personal belongings, their hair—just taken away. They were deprived of any right to privacy. An hour later, they looked at each other and burst out laughing: they all looked so odd. A week later, they had already forgotten what they looked like before.

Will we ever know what life was like for Concentration Camp Man? Will we ever understand how he could endure so long without surrendering his will to survive another night, another hour?

Will we ever understand the meaning of the phenomenon called Auschwitz or Sachsenhausen? Friends who read these words, know this: *never* will you understand what your brothers and sisters endured there.

The forced labor, the long "Roll Calls," the public floggings, the hangings, the shouts of the Kapos, the last gasps of the dying, the fixed gaze of the "Muselmaenner," the Selektion nights: never will you see what some of us have seen and witnessed. But you must learn about it. Our survival and yours is at stake. It would be a betrayal to forget: if we have survived to betray the dead, it would have been better not to have survived at all.

That is why we have never stopped shouting, reminding, whispering: "we must not forget, above all, do not forget . . . " It is easy to say. Even though it is linked to the events that occurred, it all ends up becoming blurred and indistinct. How can I be sure that I shall always remember all the emaciated faces which throng through my mind? How can I guarantee that I shall always recall the gestures, the phrases, the unfinished lives and destinies which haunted me for years and entered my harmless, easy pleasures? Once I swore: "I shall never forget!" I will continue to make that vow, I shall swear that oath. But in the depth of my being I am afraid. I am afraid of forgetting. That is why I appeal to you: "Brothers, help me. Help me not to forget." Help me to remember:

A Hassid called Jacob who chanted kaddish for all of us from morning to night: I remember him every time I in turn recite the kaddish.

A Dutch lawyer who gave a comic speech to entertain and to distract his companions one evening when there was a Selektion. It was the most wonderful address of his career. He left us next day and I am ashamed that I cannot repeat his discourse to you.

A father who shared his piece of moldy bread with his son. A son who took the blows meant for his father. People who did not know each other moving into a group as one when they sensed death sniffing around. Groups who went straight to the gas chambers, remaining unaware that Jewish chroniclers in the Sonderkommando tried desperately to report their end. Tell me, you my friends who read these words. Tell me: what should I do to include it all in our memories?

Sometimes, I wanted to open my memory wide so that it would absorb names, just names—those of the deserted ghettoes and of the overflowing cemeteries, of the camps, of the dead. I could think and say nothing but names, names, names, right to the end of my days.

Buna and Gleiwitz, do you know them? Ble-chame and Dora, Chelmno and Belzec, do you know them? The trucks of death by suffocation, the tunnels of death by exhaustion, the sites of death by hunger, the laboratories of death by so-called medical experiments, the massacres in broad daylight, the children thrown alive into burning pits: do you believe it? Tell me, my friends: do you accept in your heart and in your con-science the testimony of the witness? Well, then—how do you manage to sleep at night?

It came to pass in those days, said Rabbi Mi-chael Dov Weismandel, that normal beings had to lose their reason, and those who did not lose it—were not normal.

In those days, in those days . . .

But then, no one was what we would call "nor-mal" today. The basic laws of Creation were not in nor-mal working order. Two times two did not make four: it made six million. An entire metropolis, a country, a na-tion with its doctors and its workers, its princes and its beggars, its merchants and assistants . . . Imagine the population of a country in Europe which is swallowed up overnight with its six million inhabitants. No, do not try. You cannot imagine the unimaginable.

"They will refuse to believe you," said the kill-ers to their victims to make the suffering worse. "Even when you are dead, you do not frighten us. People will refuse to look in your direction. The few survivors will talk, but no one will believe them. They will be thought mad. They will be pitied. They will be isolated in special asylums. They will be more pitied than the dead."

Were they right? Perhaps. They were right about so many things. They said that humanity would remain indifferent to the fate of the Jews; and they were right. They predicted the tragedy of the survivors and, again, they were right. Help us, brothers, to show them that they are no longer right. That is why, at the end of these memories evoked from the past, we implore you to join us as allies. Apart, we are all condemned to a solitude too heavy to bear. Together, we can face the killers. Together, we can justify each other's existence.

Open your heart and close your eyes: beyond, on the far side of the horizon, thousands upon thousands of men, women and children walk between heaven and earth. They cannot see you, but it is important to them that you should see them. They cannot speak to you, but it is important to them that we should speak with each other. They come from the darkest exile of our history. They march toward an invisible sanctuary formed of names and letters of fire. Do not turn away from them, brothers. They are our brothers and sisters; they are our parents. They hear our promises and our visions: they are Jacob's ladder linking the Throne on high to the tragedies on earth.

Vayehi erev, vayehi voker: and it was morning and it was evening. The call follows the silence, the prayer makes the dawn more luminous and pure. Created by God on the sixth day, Adam looked at the future and his heart was filled with sadness. His head in his hands, he wanted to ask the Creator: "But why, why?" If God answered, his reply escapes us.

We only have the question. But it is we who must turn it into a prayer. A call to combat evil. A warning against indifference. A song which, in spite of everything, will try to justify the first gleam of a hope which is yet to be born.

Vayehi erev, vayehi voker:

In those days the Lord covered His face so as not to see His creation soiled, drowned in blood, and buried in ashes. Trapped, man forgot his mission and allied himself to death.

In those days, expelled from the memory cells of humanity, the Jewish people entered into darkness. In those days, God saw the annihilation of all that is human in man. In those days, to be a Jew meant to lose all rights, to be handed over to the mob. Marked, isolated, excluded from the human family, the Jew was condemned to submit, suffer, crawl, pray, and to be snuffed out like a candle in the wind.

In those days, outside the ghettoes, far from the communal graves, the people said to be our brothers lived well. They celebrated festivals and arranged weddings. While the executioners killed, the brothers and friends, the families of their victims, carried on as if nothing was happening.

We are overwhelmed when we think of those days. What was it? Indifference? Lack of feeling? Ignorance? Disbelief? How can we explain it? No explanation can satisfy.

It all hurts. It all must hurt. Vayehi erev, vayehi voker . . .

And it came to pass at that time that the days were all the same for a Jew who was being pursued, tracked down and humiliated. The nights, too. And in the street, the faces were all the same. Mistrust, spite, hate, cruelty and viciousness surrounded him, enveloped him, stifled him. He wanted to pray and study, to work so that men would be reconciled to their fate, but he no longer knew how. He wished to hide, but he did not know where. The light frightened him, the darkness protected him: he chose to live at night.

Once, in a cemetery, he encountered another fugitive, a Jew like himself. They became friends. "What did you do . . . before?" "I taught Jewish children to pray." "Really? Then heaven must have sent you to me. Teach me a prayer." "Which one?" "The kaddish." "For whom?" "For my children. For their mother. For my friends. For my illusions. For my lost years."

His friend made him recite kaddish not once but ten times. It was not the kaddish we know. We do not know, I fear that we will never know, the kaddish that two Jews recited in those days in an abandoned cemetery.

Sometimes, I even wonder if it was not kiddush which they recited. Not the kiddush we say on Friday nights here and throughout the living communities of Israel when we sanctify the wine and bless the Sabbath, but another, different kiddush: "Vayehi erev, vayehi voker—and it was evening and it was morning, Lord. Thou Who hast created the heavens and the earth, why hast Thou made them oppose each other? Why hast Thou chosen to retire to your celestial sphere when more than ever men have need of Thy presence on earth? Thou, O Lord, Who hast commanded us to keep the seventh day holy, where art Thou to receive our offering? Thou, O Lord, Who hast conferred on us faith in the week which has passed and in the one to come, why hast Thou allowed the killer to come between us and that faith, between us and Thee? Va-y'chulu hashamayim: and the heavens collapsed, and the earth as well. For God, for reasons his people do not understand, had finished his work too soon, before depriving Evil of its power . . . "

In those days, prayers got rather muddled. Spirits wandered. "Let us go," said a Jew to his friend, or to himself. "Where can we go?" "It does not matter, but let us leave this cemetery." That was not so easy. In those days, the whole earth had become a cemetery.

The whole earth? Not only the earth—the sky as well. Invisible cemeteries, monuments of ashes, to the memory of a humanity which disappeared, engulfed, swept away forever, to the memory of a people whose only wrongdoing was to want to be more human than the others and more generous.

Vayehi erev, vayehi voker . . .

And so, my fellow Jews, each episode we have recounted here stands for a thousand episodes; each name we evoked symbolizes a thousand names. You may well say that the tale you repeat—after us, with us, for us—is too vast to be included in a single book. But if all the books in the world tried to tell, they still would not succeed. Learn from this, my fellow Jews, that there are some tragedies deeper than the ocean.

Vayehi erev, vayehi voker . . .

Close your eyes, fellow Jews. Look at the sky

whose flames tear us apart and cast light upon us. Does it hurt to look at them? Does it hurt to remember? It is just a scratch, that is all. We can never remember all the days of destruction. Just a fragment. An hour. A bloody dawn. A groan at twilight. A cry of distress. An old man's silence. That should be enough.

Vayehi erev, vayehi voker . . .

A day, a night. A community. A family. A child. A mother. Lying in each other's arms. A boy and his fiancée, united in a love destroyed. A body, and another, and another. Do not weep, my fellow Jews. Above all, do not weep. That would be too easy. Let us listen to their tears which flow in us without a sound, without the slightest sound. Let us listen.

liturgies

INTRODUCTORY NOTES

TO A CHRISTIAN
IN SEARCH OF PRAYERS

How can we give you words when there are no words? *The Six Days of Destruction* open a door. You enter it of your own volition, and a heart of flesh and blood is exchanged for a heart of stone—our souls are frozen by the glimpse of hell. We must warm ourselves at the fires of our traditions, so that icy horror can give way to compassion: compassion for all who died, and for all who lived; compassion for our neighbors and for ourselves; compassion for God.

We need to pray. There are rituals in every community which serve that need. The prayers are new and old, spontaneous and commanded, open and closed to the needs of the worshiper and the community. In the decades after the Holocaust, Christianity has begun to come to terms with its greatest problem during that time: the failure of nerve which beset the Church and the Faith during those dark days. There is an agenda here of unresolved guilt, of suppressed compassion, of a flawed liturgy which permitted and encouraged antisemitism, of Christian victims who were abandoned by the Church, of a Confessing Church which was isolated, of the Jewish neighbors who were ignored. And all of this must find expression within a vital religious community in the process of growth and renewal.

How can we give you words from the outside? The affirmations of your own faith create liturgies of concern which link prayers and action. As a privileged participant in interfaith dialogue, I saw this in Brown's Chapel in Selma, Alabama, in the days when we marched behind Martin Luther King. Recently, I stood in Canterbury Cathedral and listened to a symphony orchestra and two choirs celebrating a requiem for the million Jewish children who died in the concentration camps. There is *always* room in the Christian liturgy for every possible intercession. The Dean of the Cathedral represented the concerned Christian who knows that intercessions do more than acknowledge current trouble spots on the globe where individuals are persecuted—they recognize the festering evils which have not been acknowledged and confronted, the encapsulated trauma within our society which must be opened for healing to take place. Prayer heals. They must be your prayers, your words, your encounter with God and with humanity.

We would like to think that this text will help you in your quest. *The Six Days of Destruction* are there to be read by you. In silence. Then, they may well enter the liturgy of your church. They could be read and studied during a special act of worship on Yom Ha-Shoah (Holocaust Memorial Day), in silence or aloud. They could be part of an inter-faith service, an ecumenical Christian service or as part of a small group somewhere in your sanctuary in search of truth and compassion.

We hope that this small book will enter your home. It may travel from church to home, as the prayers impel you to seek out the memory of those who died. Or the book will be studied by you in the quietness of your own home—and will then impel you to enter your sanctuary for private or communal prayer. On that day, you will be linked to many mourners; and you may feel closer to God.

We will pray alongside of you. We cannot tell you what to say, or how to say it—we will only pray that you can pray at all. We pray with you because we are concerned. We do not pray out of hatred, or in vengeance. We pray because you are also our concern, and because we care for you. We pray because we know that we have a common task. We need to remember together. We need to mourn together.

We need to live together in the past so that there may be a future. From days of destruction, we would move forward together to days of creation.

We know that the world is good.

TO A READER REJECTING PRAYER

The night was too long and too dark. The break was absolute. There are many in the Jewish tradition, in the Christian tradition, outside all religious tradition, who have lost faith and who reject faith in the days after the Holocaust. We can understand this, and will not force faith, will not demand prayer. Prayers can deceive, can make us feel that we have solved problems which are beyond solution, that we have escaped into light when we have simply blocked out the darkness. But most of us still need prayer, if only as a way to God so that we can argue with God. Challenging God is very much part of the Jewish tradition, from Abraham to Job to the doubters of our own time. And we need prayers to help us mourn.

The *Six Days of Destruction* are more than a prayer book. They are *a Memorbook,* a history of events and of persons who must be recalled by later generations. If you do not pick up this text to pray, take it as a book to be studied. It is history. Other historical works are built out of little facts which are glued together. This work begins with an ultimate reality which had to be reduced into small fictional components in order to approach our mind and our heart. Each tale ends in death. Each tale is continued in our own life and thus becomes part of a new creation. Your act of remembering will be more than many prayers that are said in the world. And if we become too strong in our assertion that the world is good, you must be part of our community to remind us that the darkness is still there.

There is evil in the world; you must not let us forget this.

TO THE JEWISH COMMUNITY

We are divided in so many things. We argue among ourselves. Theologians can speak of the dynamic tension between polarities, of the necessary struggle between conflicting approaches which help us in the search for truth. But we know that these divisions are the tragedy of Jewish life. "In their death they were not divided," sang David of Saul and Jonathan; and the Jews of Europe did die as one. But they are mourned separately. There are conflicts behind the scenes when Yom Ha-Shoah services are planned in the community. At the time of our common grief, we are often apart.

Elie Wiesel has written a text for us which can unite us. It indicates the immensity of our loss, the impossibility of matching it by our grief. Six lives end in death; six million individuals were part of a much larger column moving into the dark valley. And we must reach out toward one another to give comfort, must share the task of being remembrancers and mourners. We must do this as individuals, and we must do it as a community.

Slowly, Yom Ha-Shoah is establishing itself within Jewish life. It will differ from community to community. Israel adds the extra dimension of "g'vurah," the physical and spiritual heroism which must be remembered by us and the world. Both are recalled in this text. Again, it is a text to be read in the home, and it is a text for the synagogue. It is suitable for the long nights of study which once filled the synagogues with swaying bodies and the light and shadows of flickering candles. More than anything else, it is reading for a special day which will unite all Jewry, even all of us scattered to the four corners of the world. Let it serve as the impetus for a special service. Written in diverse languages, it will yet unite us as we ponder the same thoughts on the same day from the same text. In order to draw us closer together at this time, we have added a liturgy for the Jewish community to this edition. We would welcome its use by any other community; we would understand and appreciate the need of many Jewish congregations to see this text as one possible model and move toward their own statements of affirmation. Songs may awaken in the night to accompany the text; or it may be enfolded in silence. Whatever response is evoked, let us remember that behind all our words is the reality of the time of destruction; and that, ahead of us, lies the time of creation.

Guidelines for the Use of *The Six Days of Destruction* in Christian Worship Services

When this text was completed, a number of consultations took place between the editor and members of the Christian communities in Great Britain and the United States. The Deans of Westminster and St. Paul, Bishop Harries of Oxford, and the thoughts of Krister Stendahl on Holy Week preaching were particularly helpful. The following suggestions emerged out of this dialogue:

1. The Christian community will find this text particularly helpful for the Lenten season. On various occasions, Bishop Stendahl has preached on the Holocaust on Good Friday and has pointed out (*Holy Week Preaching*, Fortress Press, pp. 9ff) that "we must uproot every possible plant of anti-Semitism from our celebration of Holy Week . . . the suffering that Christians . . . have piled up on the Jews—our celebration of Holy Week must be one of repentance." Using this text as a sermon resource or as basic reading for a study session within the community would bring new

awareness of Christian teachings of repentance central to the observances of Holy Week. The Lenten season precedes *Yom Ha-Shoah*, and the themes of pain, suffering and repentance are enunciated in it. How can the thinking Christian ignore the Holocaust during this period?

2. Building upon this insight, Dr. Richard Harries (former Dean of King's College in London and now bishop of Oxford) suggests that Passion Sunday should be the regular observance of the Holocaust in the Christian liturgy. Since *Yom Ha-Shoah* is bound to the movable Jewish lunar calendar, it would be more natural for Christians to join their Jewish friends in communal observances within the Jewish community, but place their own specific observances into their Lenten season of anguish and repentance. Passion Sunday, toward the end of Lent, brings the Christian community to the contemplation of the way ahead, when the Christian tries to act upon the insights gained during the period of self-examination. The task of remembering the Holocaust and Christian responsibility, of healing wounds and striving for reconciliation, can give new meaning to Passion Sunday.

The specific suggestions here call for a use of "Six Days of Destruction" within the Christian liturgy of Passion Sunday. It might be used at the close of the evening service. The minister would say a few words of introduction, and the congregation would spend the next ten minutes quietly reading one of the stories of destruction. Then the liturgy given here could be used—either as is or in a shortened version. A rabbi could be invited to participate. Otherwise, the minister and members of the congregation could read the liturgy. One suggestion is that the youth group of the church could present the text. A closing word could also be given by a visitor—survivor, rabbi, Christian scholar of the Holocaust, etc.—and the service could be adapted as needed. The most important aspect of this use of the Holocaust is to place it firmly into the

Christian liturgy. As the *regular* observance during the Lenten season, it would be the particular Christian memorial which would stand alongside *Yom Ha-Shoah* but would be independent of it.

If communal interfaith services are planned by the Christian communities, it must be remembered that the Holocaust continues to be the most sensitive area of contact between Jews and their neighbors. The local rabbi and members of the Jewish community must be included in the first planning sessions. This should start many months in advance—some problem always emerges which needs time to be resolved. And, clearly, *The Six Days of Destruction* are not the final word on a theme where no words suffice. In this context, it is a question asked of the Christian community, waiting for an answer of compassion and concern.

The Haggadah—the Passover liturgy of this season when the most profound Christian and Jewish prayers are very close and very far from each other—records a conversation among the rabbis:

> Rabbi Eleazar ben Azariah said, "I am now over 70 years old; but I never understood why the story of Exodus has to be recited by night until Ben Zoma expounded it thus: The Torah (Deut. 16:3) states: 'that thou mayest remember the day when thou camest out of the land of Egypt *all* the days of thy life.' 'The days of thy life' might imply the days only; 'all the days of thy life' includes the nights as well!"

We cannot exclude the nights, the dark and recurrent passages in life where we encounter terror and pain. And we cannot edit that terror and remember only part of it. The Christian Lenten season, that time of remembrance and remorse, must not exclude the suffering of its neighbor from its liturgies. Remembering the past, praying for each other, we come to pray together. In that encounter, we encounter God.

a service for Jewish communities

(This is a model of a service for communities observing Yom Ha-Shoah. It can be introduced into any standard service, although the service is basically visualized as an evening service. Any place of assembly and any House of Worship is suitable for this commemoration. The congregation should enter into darkness, illuminated by candles or dim lights. In front, there should be a Shoah candelabra, with the six lights already lit. (Alternative: the leader lights a taper, hands it to a child to light the six candles. All is done in silence.)

Music: Ani maamin (quietly, either by cantor or instrumental music).

Reader: (moves forward as the music ceases):

We begin—with silence.
The silence of death; the silence of life.
The silence after destruction;
The silence before creation.
There are times when songs falter,
When darkness fills life,
When martyrdom becomes a constellation of faith
Against the unrelieved black of space about us.
There are no words to reach beyond the edge of night,
No messengers to tell the full tale.
There is only silence.

The silence of Job.
The silence of the Six Million.
The silence of memory.
Let us remember them as we link our silences
Into the silence which becomes a prayer,
Which links us with the past,
Touching that darkness we cannot fully enter,
The anguish which is memory; and love.
And life and death.

(Six minutes of silence follow during which congregants may wish to read one of the six chronicles.)

Reader: Silence leads to memories. Memories become words. Words become images:

The world of Eastern Europe rises before us, thousands upon thousands of little children learning Torah; homes in which the Sabbath candles burned, streets where walkers argued points of law and where the outside world was far away. There was poverty; and lack of vision, too. But there was a depth and a greatness which we have no longer; and we weep for what is lost.

And there was Western Europe, where Jewish life had flowered into a golden period of creativity: scholars, poets, merchants, artists and musicians joined ancient and modern visions in a joyous celebration of life. The world had a special glow, and genius resided within that Jewry. Then—creation was followed by destruction.

There was the Sephardic world, as well: a pious culture, a quiet and enduring way of Jewish life; a thousand years of scholarship, of family life and joy. In Athens and Salonika, in the mellah and on the isles of the Mediterranean, Jews prayed to God and trusted their neighbours. And that world also ceased.

Darkness covered the Jewish world. Fire burned the books and the buildings. Night and fog swallowed up the people on their way to death. We weep for them, we yearn for them now. We reach toward them through the stories of lives, by reciting names: Chavah, Sarah, Itzikl, Yehuda—their names, their lives, are intertwined with ours. They are part of our collective memories, of our history: the Warsaw Ghetto alongside the Walls of Jerusalem; the musicians of Auschwitz and the still harps at the waters of Babylon; the murdered temple singers and the children of Terezin. They speak to us softly, from Babi Yar and from the transports:

New Reader: Written in Pencil on the Sealed Railway Car:
here in this carload
i eve
with abel my son
if you see my other son
cain son of man
tell him i . . . . . . " (Dan Pagis, *Selected Poems*)

Reader: (waits for a moment):Silence. Only silence. Waiting for our reply. All of them, waiting. Three million and three hundred thousand Jews lived in Poland before the war.

Congregation: Three million died.

Reader: Two million eight hundred and fifty thousand Jews lived in Russia.

Congregation: More than a million died.

Reader: One and a half million Jews lived in the Balkans and Slavic countries.

Congregation: More than a million died.

Reader: Germany, Austria, France and Italy had six hundred and fifty thousand Jews.

Congregation: Half of them died.

Reader: Rhodes and Cyprus had happy, thriving congregations.

Congregation: The synagogues stand empty, now.

Reader: Our brothers and sisters were murdered everywhere in the days of destruction.

Congregation: They died in cities and towns, in villages and fields.

Reader: They died in the night and the fog, they died between dawn and dusk.

Congregation: They died by fire and water, by poison and gun.

Reader: They died alone; but we will not forget them.

Congregation: They died alone; but we will not forget them.

Reader: We will remember them; in reverence, and in silence.

(A period of silence follows, for private memories, for reading one of the stories of *The Six Days of Destruction,* or for quiet meditation. The silence is ended by the following song which may be sung by the congregation or a soloist, or played without singing.)

Zog Nit Keyn Mol!

Words by Hirsh Glik

Zog nit kein-mol az du geist dem letz-tn veg.
pal-men land biz vai-tu land fun shnei,

Ven him-len blai-e-ne far shte-in bloi-e teg.
Mir ku-men on mit un-zer pain mit un-zer vei.

Ku-men vet noch un-zer ois-ge-benk-te sho,
Vu ge-fa-ln s'iz a shpritz fun un-zer blut,

S'vet a poik ton un-zer trot mir zai-nen do.
Shpro-tzn vet dort un-zer gvu-re un-zer mut.

Ku-men vet noch un-zer ois-ge-benk te sho,
Vu ge-fa-ln s'iz a shpritz fun un-zer blut,

S'vet a poik ton un-zer trot mir zai-nen do. Fun gri-nem
Shpro-tzn vet dort un-zer gvu-re un-zer mut.

Reader: They fought; and they died. The individuals. The communities.

Far, far
A city lies. Body still warm.
Bells are ringing.

You have not seen a city thrust on its back
like a horse in its blood, jerking its hooves
unable to rise.

Bells are ringing.

City.
City.
How mourn a city
whose people are dead and whose dead are
    alive
in the heart.

Bells.   (Abba Kovner, *My Little Sister*)

A Reader: Reports, letters to the living, from those who fought in the ghettos and in the forests. Abba Kovner had led his people in the Vilna ghetto and in the partisan woods. And the fight for his people continued in the land of Israel. Others sent letters to God, and brought them to him in person. Poets cried out their anguish. And the empty land shook in pain. Across that landscape, iron rails gave mute testimony of trains which had passed over it, of carriages seen by everyone and by no one.

Congregation: Confess, O empty wagons: Whence? Where? Confess!

Reader: Now? Now? As wagons
You roll on.
And see the pain.
Madness reverberates.
Mute witnesses, you know
The needs and pain of every terror-night.

You know what happens:
Confess, mute ones, where you roll!
For it is death you serve.
My people, my Jewish people,
Where have you taken them?

Congregation: You are not guilty.
You are crammed to bursting,
And then the butcher shouts: Away!
He sends you out into the unknown: full.
And? Empty you return.

Turn, wheels. Tell, tell.
As for me: tears dim my vision. (Y. Katze-
nelson, *Song of the Last Jew*, song four,
"Again the wagons wait for us . . .")

Reader: Blinded by our tears, we cannot see.
Blinded by our grief, we cannot believe.
But beyond grief, beyond belief,
gently, gently, there is the whisper of a
night-song,
of an affirmation which could not be
slain . . .

ani maamin, softly (music, either solo voice or
solo instrument)

Reader: Ani maamin, Abraham,
Despite Treblinka,
Ani maamin, Isaac,
Because of Belsen.
Ani Maamin, Jacob,
Because and in spite of Majdanek.

Congr.: Dead in vain,
Dead for naught,
Ani maamin.
Pray, men.
Pray to God,
Against God,
For God.
Ani maamin.

Reader: Whether the Messiah comes,
Ani maamin.
Or is late in coming,
Ani maamin.
Whether God is silent
Or weeps,
Ani maamin.

Congr.: Ani maamin for him,
In spite of him.
I believe in You,
Even against your will.
Even if you punish me
For believing in You.

Reader: Blessed are the fools
Who shout their faith.
Blessed are the fools
Who go on laughing,
Who mock the man who mocks the Jew,
Who help their brothers
Singing over and over and over:

Congr.: Ani Maamin, ani maamin beviat ha-
Mashiah, v'af al pi she-yitmameha,
Akhake lo bekhol yom she-yava, Ani
Maamin! (Elie Wiesel, *Ani Maamin*).

Reader: Our belief will lead us from the destruction
to the creation;
our unbelief will guard us against compla-
cency, against forgetting,
will challenge our idolatry of little gods:

A Reader: A Psalm by Paul Celan

Congr.: No-one kneads us again out of earth and
clay,
No-one bespeaks our dust.
No-one.
Praised art Thou, No-One.
For your sake we want
To flower.

Unto
Thee.

Reader: Our belief will lead us from the destruction
to the creation;
our unbelief will guard us against compla-
cency, against forgetting,
will challenge our idolatry of little gods:

A Reader: A Psalm by Paul Celan
A nothing
Were we, are we, will
We remain, flowering:
The nothing—, the
No-one's rose.

Reader: The mystery of the En-Sof, of God Who is
near and Who is far, Who may at times be
absent, is always with us. It has been said:
"When God's back is towards man, history
is Auschwitz" (G. Steiner). Yet in every age
there have been those who still reached out
to God, the mothers of Israel protecting their
children, the fathers pleading with God. The
Rav of Slobodka, the girls of the ghetto, the
steadfastness of the teachers in the camps is
Israel, wrestling with God in the darkness,
and prevailing.

A Reader: A liturgical meditation of our time:
When Leo Baeck came out of the black mid-
night of the concentration camp, he looked
about at the world and at his neighbors.
Many averted their eyes. They had been silent. They had been selfish—or they had followed the multitude to do evil. In the
darkness of the camps, Leo Baeck had not
despaired. He had fulfilled his function: he
had taught and he had given comfort. And,
in the darkness of the new world which had
to live with the memory of Belsen and
Auschwitz, Baeck continued to teach and to

comfort his people. They say that when Baeck lifted his hands and spoke the priestly benediction the congregation felt very close to the Divine Presence. "May the Lord look kindly upon you and be gracious to you"— these words took on new meaning for the worshippers. In ancient times, the image of one Babylonian god was a clay furnace. When the fires of human sacrifice burned high, the eyes of the idol glared death upon the onlookers. To see God was to die. Biblical Israel transformed the terror into awe, and fear became love. In God's light we saw light. But in our days, the world grew dark again. The pagan furnace roared, and Israel ascended into the sky as smoke. And we who are alive wander across a darkened landscape fitfully illuminated by burning idols in which some exterminate their human kin.

We need our teachers: those who died for the sanctification of the Divine Name, and those who lived to guide and comfort us. They tell us that the encounter with God can take place in the utmost darkness—if we are ready for it. The blessing that shone through Leo Baeck can touch our lives: "May God look upon us and give us peace." (from *Gates of Prayer*)

(*Music:* Ha-shivenu eley-cha v'na-shuvah)

Reader and Congregation: Return us, O God, to our task and to our people.

Renew our days as of old, bring back the time of creation.

Return us to our neighbors, to those who have suffered with us,

to those who still live in darkness, to those who need our help.

Return us, and renew us.

Reader: All of life is return and renewal, is creation
after destruction.

Akiva walked alongside the Temple Mount,
and saw the jackals playing

among the ruins. And he sensed a divine
plan of darkness and light, of

a land to be restored, of a people to be returned to God. Our survivors

belong to the company of Akiva. We honor
and revere them. We are their

students. How can we feel what they feel?
How can we know what they know?

All we can do is to take their silence.

And we can take their words.

And interweave past and present, present
and future.

And we can pray. And hope.

Congr.: Six million names come to us out of the destruction.

In a world where there was no compassion,
we turn to the God of Compassion.

They are bound up with our lives. May they
be bound up in the bundle of

eternal life, among the Holy and the Pure
who shine so brightly in the

firmament of our lives:

El Mole Rachamim is chanted and recited:

MEMORIAL PRAYER

אֵל מָלֵא רַחֲמִים שׁוֹכֵן בַּמְּרוֹמִים. הַמְצֵא מְנוּחָה נְכוֹנָה תַּחַת
כַּנְפֵי הַשְּׁכִינָה בְּמַעֲלוֹת קְדוֹשִׁים וּטְהוֹרִים. כְּזוֹהַר הָרָקִיעַ
מַזְהִירִים. לְנִשְׁמוֹת שִׁשָּׁה מִלְיוֹן אַחֵינוּ וְאַחְיוֹתֵינוּ שֶׁמֵּתוּ עַל־
קִדּוּשׁ הַשֵּׁם. יָנוּחוּ בַשַּׁלְוָה וּבַשָּׁלוֹם שֶׁלֹּא יָדְעוּ בְחַיֵּיהֶם. בְּעַל
הָרַחֲמִים הַסְתִּירֵם בְּסֵתֶר כְּנָפֶיךָ לְעוֹלָמִים. וּצְרוֹר בִּצְרוֹר הַחַיִּים
אֶת־נִשְׁמָתָם. יְיָ הוּא נַחֲלָתָם וְיָנוּחוּ בְשָׁלוֹם עַל מִשְׁכָּבָם. וְנֹאמַר
אָמֵן:

God full of compassion whose presence is over us, may the souls of our six million dead who have gone to their everlasting home with the holy and pure on high who shine as the lights of heaven, find the safety and rest denied them on earth beneath the shelter of Your presence. Master of mercy, cover them in the shelter of Your wings forever, and bind their souls into the gathering of life. It is the Lord who is their heritage. May they be at peace in their place of rest. Amen.

Reader: Creation follows destruction, and destruction follows creation. We lit six candles tonight to commemorate our dead. Soon, these candles will flicker and die, and return to darkness. Soon, we begin to forget—and we must not let this happen. Let us kindle one more light, a Yahrzeit candle to which we return each season; and let us recite the prayer of praise which the poet intertwined with the memory of suffering. Let us say Kaddish.

(Yahrzeit candle lit on pulpit, Kaddish recited by all:)

Congregation rises

Yit-gadal	יִתְגַּדַּל
Lodz	Lodz
ve-yit-kadash	וְיִתְקַדַּשׁ
Gurs	Gurs
shmei raba	שְׁמֵהּ רַבָּא,
Warsaw	Warsaw
b'alma divra khri'atei	בְּעָלְמָא דִּי בְרָא כִרְעוּתֵהּ,
Bogdanovka	Bogdanovka
ve-yamlikh mal-khutei	וְיַמְלִיךְ מַלְכוּתֵהּ
Ravensbruck	Ravensbruck
be-hayei-kohn uve'yomei-khon	בְּחַיֵּיכוֹן וּבְיוֹמֵיכוֹן
Vilna	Vilna

uve-hayei di-khol beit yisrael	וּבְחַיֵּי דְכָל בֵּית יִשְׂרָאֵל
Treblinka	Treblinka
b-agala u-vizmon kariv	בַּעֲגָלָא וּבִזְמַן קָרִיב,
Chelmno	Chelmno
v'imru amen	וְאִמְרוּ אָמֵן.
Ye-hei shmei rabo mevo-rach	יְהֵא שְׁמֵהּ רַבָּא מְבָרַךְ
l'olam ul'olmei olma-ya	לְעָלַם וּלְעָלְמֵי עָלְמַיָּא.
Yit-barakh ve-yish-tabah	יִתְבָּרַךְ וְיִשְׁתַּבַּח
Belzec	Belzec
ve-yit-pa-ar ve-yitromam	וְיִתְפָּאַר וְיִתְרוֹמַם
Buchenwald	Buchenwald
ve-yitnasei ve-yit hador	וְיִתְנַשֵּׂא וְיִתְהַדָּר
Sobibor	Sobibor
ve-yit'aleh ve-yit-halal	וְיִתְעַלֶּה וְיִתְהַלָּל
Maidanek	Maidanek
shmei di-kudsha brikh hu	שְׁמֵהּ דְּקֻדְשָׁא בְּרִיךְ הוּא,
Mauthausen	Mauthausen
l'eila	לְעֵלָּא
Babi'yar	Babi Yar
mikol bir-khata ve-shirata	מִכָּל בִּרְכָתָא וְשִׁירָתָא,
Bergen-Belsen	Bergen-Belsen
tush-be-hata ve-nehe-mata	תֻּשְׁבְּחָתָא וְנֶחֱמָתָא
Dachau	Dachau
da-amiran b'alma	דַּאֲמִירָן בְּעָלְמָא.
Auschwitz	Auschwitz
v'imru amen.	וְאִמְרוּ אָמֵן.
Ye-hei shlama raba min	יְהֵא שְׁלָמָא רַבָּא מִן
shmaya ve-hayim aleinu v'al	שְׁמַיָּא וְחַיִּים עָלֵינוּ וְעַל כָּל
kol yisrael v'imru amen.	יִשְׂרָאֵל, וְאִמְרוּ אָמֵן.
Oseh shalom bimromav	עֹשֶׂה שָׁלוֹם בִּמְרוֹמָיו,
hu ya'aseh	הוּא יַעֲשֶׂה
shalom aleinu v'al kol	שָׁלוֹם עָלֵינוּ וְעַל כָּל
yisrael v'imru amen.	יִשְׂרָאֵל, וְאִמְרוּ אָמֵן.

Reader: Amen v'amen. The service has finished; and
our task has begun. Quietly, let us go home.

(Participants walk out quietly)

an interreligious service

From Death to Hope

by

Eugene J. Fisher and Leon Klenicki

The service begins in silence and in darkness as the narrators, readers and choir enter in procession. Slowly the lights are turned on.

The narrator stands on one side, a podium for readers on the other. The readers are seated near this podium. Readers can be chosen to light the candles, or others from the community can go up to light the candles at the appropriate time.

Narrator

We begin our service in remembrance of the Holocaust in silence. Let us surround our worship, our community in prayer, with silence, silence in preparation for the Presence of God.

Silent Meditation

Silence does not just bring to a standstill words and noise. Silence is more than the temporary renunciation of speech. It is a door opening before prayer, toward the very realms of the spirit and the heart. Silence is the beginning of a reckoning of the soul, the prelude to an account of the past and the consideration of the present. May our shared silence lead us to awareness of a time of total evil that degraded our most precious values, the very meaning of religious existence, and life itself. Our silence is to be a committed accounting for other silences, that accepted persecutions and were indifferent to debasement and crime. For there *was* a time when silence was a crime. We think particularly of one night of silence, half a century ago: *Kristallnacht,* the Night of Broken Crystals, the 9th of November, 1938. Then, all the synagogues in Germany rose up in flame and smoke to the skies. The churches next to them stood in darkness, and in silence. Glass littered the streets—the broken shop-windows of the Jewish community. The neighbors walked upon the crunching splinters and were silent. A few prayed. Some churches courageously expressed their grief. But a dark cloud of silence filled the world. When will that silence end? When will we speak out on behalf of suffering neighbors? Not until we affirm God together; not until we acknowledge that we are all God's children. From the silence of uncaring, let us move on to the silence which is the search for God, the search within ourselves. Then we can move beyond that silence: we can affirm the One God, we can proclaim God's Name to the world! *(congregation stands)*

Reader: Praise and proclaim God's Name, to whom all praise is due!

Congregation: Praised and proclaimed be the Name of God, to whom all praise is due, now and forever! *(congregation is seated)*

Narrator: Out of silence, out of darkness, the creative Word of God was spoken. It first took the form of wind, of *ruach*, God's spirit hovering over the waters of chaos to control them, to hold them back and make possible the goodness of creation itself. Through the millennia, the process has continued, as humanity came to share in the work of creation. Days of light and nights of darkness were linked together. We turn back to those days of creation; and we link them with the days of destruction in our time, so that the *ruach* of God may drive back the darkness and give us light.

Reader: In the beginning of God's creating the heaven and the earth, the earth was without form and void. And darkness hovered over the face of the deep. And the spirit of God moved upon the face of the waters. And God said: let there be light: and there was light. And God saw the light, that it was good; and God divided the light from the darkness. And God called the light Day, and the darkness he called Night. And it was evening and it was morning: the first day.

2nd Reader: *(congregation joins in):* Lord God of Creation, we thank you for the light and for the darkness, for the dark flame which engraved your letters into the firmament of creation, for the unending light shining out of the Six Days of Creation. O Lord our God, help us to find that light again in the Days of Destruction. Your daughter Hava looked for it in vain. It was swept up as shards on the streets on a night of crystal, it was lost in the chambers of advocates who killed souls with stamps. There was no shining in the skylights of the cattle-trains. It was dark there. Yet somewhere, underneath the shells pushed back and forth in cruel sport, the light is shining. Break the shells, O Lord; let the light come forth. And help us to remember those who moved from light to darkness. We praise You, Lord, Giver of light and darkness.

Reader: And God said: Let the earth bring forth living creatures, each of their kind, cattle and creeping things, beasts of the earth . . . and it was good. And God said: let us make humanity in our image, after our likeness, and let it have dominion over all . . . in God's image, male and female created He them. And God blessed them . . . and God saw everything that He had made, and behold, it was very good. And it was evening and it was morning, the sixth day.

Reader and Congregation: Then came the destruction. O Lord, how we have fallen. In the night of Sobidor, Treblinka, Birkenau, we have forgotten Your blessing. We have lost our identity; but we have been cursed with memories. O Lord, what will happen to us and to the world when the days of destruction are finished? Will the *kiddush* of rest become the final *kaddish*? Will this world end? Will a new world begin?

We do not demand answers, God. But if this

is the last page of the human chronicles, assure us that we had the right to ask. And we will always glorify Your Name: *yitgadal v'yitkadash sh'may rabba*. . . .

Reader: These Hebrew words which glorify the Name of God come from the Jewish tradition, from a people which have emerged from the *Shoah*, that devastating, diabolic wind which scoured Europe and left death and desolation in its wake, a chaos of destruction. Six million Jewish men and women, one million children among them, were taken into the death chambers to die in gas of fire. Others died alongside them:

Narrator

Not only did Jews die; caught in the eddies and swirls of the Holocaust, millions of Poles and Gypsies, Russians and other Europeans also ended their lives as victims of Nazism's diabolically efficient technology of death. But to be Jewish in Nazi Europe of itself meant alienation and death.

Reader

Martin Niemoeller, a pastor in the German Confessing Church, spent 8¹/₂ years in a concentration camp. He wrote:

> First they came for the Communists
> and I did not speak out—
> because I was not a Communist.
>
> Then they came for the Socialists
> and I did not speak out—
> because I was not a Socialist.
>
> Then they came for the trade unionists
> and I did not speak out—
> because I was not a trade unionist.
>
> Then they came for the Jews
> and I did not speak out—
> because I was not a Jew.

Then they came for me—
and there was no one left
to speak out for me.

Reader
Pope John Paul II, a Pole who knew well the heel of Nazi inhumanity, prayed during his pilgrimage to Auschwitz in 1979:

I kneel before all the inscriptions that come one after another bearing the memory of the victims of Oswiecim . . . In particular I pause with you, dear participants in this encounter, before the inscription in Hebrew. This inscription awakens the memory of the people whose sons and daughters were intended for total extermination. This people draws its origin from Abraham, our father in faith as was expressed by Paul of Tarsus. The very people who received from God the commandment "thou shalt not kill," itself experiences in a special measure what is meant by killing. It is not permissible for anyone to pass by this inscription with indifference.

THE LIGHTING OF THE MEMORIAL CANDLES

Narrator
We now light six candles in memory of the six million. As we light these candles, we commit ourselves to responsibility for one another, to build on this earth a world that has no room for hatred, no place for violence. Together, we pray for the strength to fulfill this vocation.

(Congregation stands)

(Representatives of the community light the candles. While they are being lit, the community joins in praying Psalm 22.)

Psalm 22

Congregation: My God, my God,
why have You abandoned me;
why so far from delivering me
and from my anguished roaring?

Reader: My God,
I cry by day—You answer not;
by night, and have no respite.

Congregation: But You are the Holy One,
enthroned, the Praise of Israel.
In You our fathers trusted;
they trusted and You rescued them.
To you they cried out
and they escaped;
in You they trusted
and were not disappointed.

(Congregation be seated)

TESTIMONIES

Narrator
Jewish voices were heard in reciting prayers and biblical texts, on the trains to the concentration camps, at the doors of the gas chambers, in hiding, in fighting the enemy, manifesting grief, hope, despair, trust in God, faith.

One of those voices, Moshe Flinker, an adolescent hiding in Belgium, expressed his religious fervor and commitment in verse and prayer. One afternoon he wrote in his diary.

Reader
"I am sitting at the window and readying myself for the Minha prayer, I look out, and I see that all is red, and the whole horizon is red. The sky is covered with bloody clouds, and I am frightened when I see it. I say to myself: 'Where do these clouds come from? Bleeding clouds,

where are you from?' Suddenly everything is clear to me, everything is simple and easily understood. Don't you know? They come from the seas of blood. These seas have been brought about by millions of Jews who have been captured and who knows where they are? 'We are the bleeding clouds, and from the seas of blood have we come. We have come to you from the place where your brothers are, to bring greetings from your people. We are witnesses; we were sent by your people to show you their troubles. We have come from the seas of blood: we were brought into being by an inferno of suffering, and we are a sign of peace to you' . . . "

Young Moshe who died in Auschwitz was able to find hope in his faith in God, and in the continuity of Jewish peoplehood:

Narrator	*Congregation*
A Jew in thought	A Jew in deeds
A Jew in trouble	A Jew in joy
A Jew in speech	A Jew in silence
A Jew in arising	A Jew in sitting
A Jew in God	A Jew in people
A Jew in life	A Jew in death
A Jew you were born	A Jew you will die.

(Congregation stands)

Hear, O Israel

Gregory Norbet, O.S.B.

Hear, O Is - ra - el,____ the Lord, our God,_ the Lord is one. Hear, O Is - ra -

el,_____ the Lord, our God,_ the Lord_ is

one.   Hear, O   Is - ra - el._____

Last time

el._____   Hear, O   Is - ra - el._____

Soloist

Two thou - sand years   have we been in ex - ile.

Two thou - sand years   have we been suf - fer - ing.

Two thou - sand years   have we been hop - ing for our

long - de - layed   sal - va - tion.

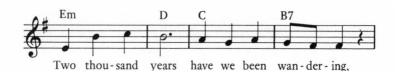

Two thou-sand years have we been wan-der-ing,

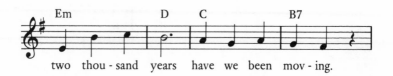

two thou-sand years have we been mov-ing.

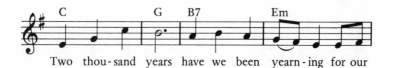

Two thou-sand years have we been yearn-ing for our

long - de - layed sal - va - tion, and

now we are stand - ing here._____ *to Chorus*

Verses

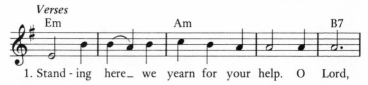

1. Stand-ing here_ we yearn for your help. O Lord,

shall_ you help____ us? Yes, our Lord_ shall

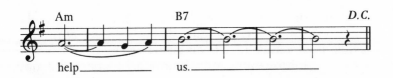

help_____ us._____

2. Yes, our re-deem-er, you shall re-deem. You have for-

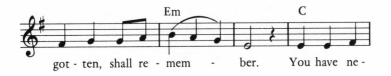

got-ten, shall re-mem - ber. You have ne-

glect-ed and you__ shall re-turn._____

Narrator
Christian witness, in this time of degradation, was
barely heard. While many were silent, some spoke with
their deeds. Let us listen now to a few of their stories.

     (One or more of the following selections may be
chosen.)

From Germany

Bernard Lichtenberg was a priest at the St. Hedwig Cathedral Church in Berlin. In August, 1941, he declared

in a sermon that he would include Jews in his daily prayers because "synagogues have been set afire and Jewish businesses have been destroyed."

One evening Monsignor Lichtenberg did not appear at his church. A brief announcement in the newspapers informed his followers that he had been arrested for "subversive activities." He was sent to prison and, after serving his term, sent to a concentration camp for "re-education." A poor student, so far as the Nazis were concerned, the ailing old priest asked to be deported to the Jewish ghetto of Lodz. His plea was ignored. He died November 3, 1943, on the way to Dachau.

From Poland

Abraham H. Foxman was born in Poland in 1940, a few months after the Germans had occupied the country. His parents fled to Vilna in an effort to keep ahead of the Nazis. But in less than a year, the German armies occupied Vilna and rounded up all Jews in a ghetto, the first step toward shipping them to concentration camps. A maid, Bronislawa Kurpi, offered to hide the baby, and within a few months he had a new name and baptismal certificate. His mother and father were together in the Vilna ghetto for one year when his mother escaped, managed to get false papers, and moved in with the maid as her sister and the baby's aunt. His father, liberated in 1945, made his way back to Vilna and his family. The whole family was smuggled out of Poland to a displaced persons' camp in the American zone of Austria. They reached the United States in 1950 when Abe was ten years old.

From Denmark

Dr. Aage Bertelsen was a pedagogue. Principal of Aarhus Cathedral College and an outstanding biblical scholar, he had shunned politics before the outbreak of the war. With his wife Gerda and several friends, Bertelsen formed a rescue organization that eventually numbered sixty people. Known as the Lyngby Group, after the town in which it operated, these modern Vikings who struck only at night smuggled 1,200 Jews past a flotilla of German warships depositing them safely on Swedish shores. Eventually the Germans learned of Bertelsen's operations and surrounded his home. But Bertelsen successfully eluded the Gestapo noose, slipped out of town, and continued to direct the rescue operations from hiding places. Finally he was forced to escape to Sweden. The Germans arrested his wife Gerda, but she refused to divulge any of the group's secrets. In reply to the bludgeoning Gestapo official who pressed her to confess that she had participated in the smuggling of Jews to Sweden, the gallant woman asserted: *"All* decent people do!"

From Belgium

In May, 1943, Mme. Marthe De Smet of Dilbeek, in the countryside near Brussels, received a telephone call from Sr. Claire, a nun at the Couvent des Soeurs du Très St. Sauveur in the city. Was she willing to hide another Jewish child, the caller asked.

The situation was desperate. The nuns had hidden fifteen little Jewish girls until their hiding place was betrayed to the Gestapo. Just hours before the Gestapo's truck arrived to take the children to their death, the nuns had somehow gotten word to the underground. The children had been hastily moved under cover of darkness and then placed in safe but temporary homes. Now, it was essential to find a permanent hiding place for each of them.

Sr. Claire knew that the De Smets—Georges, his wife, Marthe, and their children, Marie-Paule, André, Eliane and Francis—were already hiding a Jewish child, three-year-old Regine Monk. Nonetheless, she was confident that Mme. De Smet would not turn her down. She was right. A few days later, three-year-old Yvette Lerner came into the De Smet household, to be safely sheltered there until the liberation of Brussels in September, 1944. Shortly after her arrival, the De Smets took a third child, then an infant, Liliane Klein.

At the risk of their own lives and those of their children, the De Smets embarked on a course of active opposition to the Nazis' plan for the extermination of all Jews. In this, they were motivated by deep religious conviction and by a strong love of children.

After the war, the De Smets refused all remuneration and asked only for the continued friendship of the families to whom they had given so much.

From France

Important rescue work was carried on by a Catholic missionary organization, the Fathers of Our Lady of Zion . . . At the head of this group was the Reverend Father Superior Charles Devaux, who is credited with saving 443 Jewish children and 500 adults. At the end of 1942, Father Devaux organized a temporary shelter for his wards on Rue Notre Dame de Champs. From here he sent the children to many parts of the country, where they found temporary homes with workmen's families, among peasants, in convents and monasteries. The expenses were provided for by the group. When the relief work grew beyond their modest means, they solicited and received money from individuals, Jews and non-Jews alike, and from various organizations. The Gestapo were irked by the clergyman's ceaseless activities on behalf of the Jews. They summoned Father Devaux and cited a long list of his offenses. Theodore Dannecker, an SS officer noted as a hangman of French Jews, personally dealt with Devaux. He slapped the priest's face as an initial warning, and cautioned him to cease helping

Jews or accept the consequences. Father Devaux returned to his rescue work. In 1945, the brave priest was interviewed by a Jewish journalist who asked him whether he had not been aware of the great danger involved in his rescue activities. Father Devaux's answer was simple: "Of course I knew it, but this knowledge could not stop me from doing what I considered to be my duty as a Christian and a human being."

From Italy

The city of Assisi, home of St. Francis, turned itself into a place of clandestine refuge for Jews. Organized by a priest of peasant stock, Padre Rufino Niccacci, hundreds of Jews were hidden in the town's ancient monasteries and convents and provided with fake identity papers. The Germans raided the religious houses searching for the Jewish refugees, who were dressed in religious habits, given rosaries, and temporarily transformed into monks and nuns piously saying their prayers. A small printing press in the town's pharmacy at night cranked out false documents which were then smuggled to Jewish survivors throughout Italy. In all, 32,000 Italian Jews, representing 80% of Italian Jewry, and thousands of foreign Jews were hidden successfully by Christians, many in religious houses.

From Holland

After the Nazi invasion of Holland, a farm which trained Jewish youths in agriculture prior to sending them to Palestine formed a youth underground to smuggle Jewish children across the Pyrenees to Spain and from there to Palestine. But the Jews needed help and appealed to the Dutch Socialist underground. Among those who offered their assistance was a man named Joop Westerville, a principal in a Lundsrecht high school. Son of a pastor, Westerville was a noted educator, the father of three children, a fourth on the way—he was eager for his first journey across the many borders bristling with Nazi bayonets.

Early in 1943, Shushu Simon, the leader of the Jewish underground, was captured by the Gestapo. Joop Westerville was thrust into the position of leadership. It was now his job to lead the Jewish children across the Low Countries and mountainous peaks of France and Spain. This became part of his everyday existence, and he dedicated himself to it fully. At the foot of the Pyrenees where he usually took leave of the young Zionist pioneers, Westerville enjoined them not to forget their non-Jewish comrades, and reminded them that they were all bound to humanity.

Narrator

A popular Yiddish song expressed the Jewish people's determination to stand up in the struggle against the oppressor, and to affirm and reaffirm Judaism's covenant with God. *Zog nit keyn mol* is an example of human affirmation that can inspire us today. Let us read together the English translation.

Narrator and Congregation

> So never say you now go on your last way,
> Though darkened skies may now conceal the blue of day,
> Because the hour for which we've hungered is so near,
> Beneath our feet the earth shall thunder, "We are here!"

Congregation Sings

> Zog nit keyn mol as du geyst dem letstn veg
> Khotsh himlen blayene farshteln bloye teg.
> Kumen vet nokh undzer oysgebenkte sho,
> S'vet a poyk ton undzer trot—MIR ZAINEN DO!

Zog Nit Keyn Mol!

(Hymn of the Vilna Partisans)

Words by Hirsh Glik

March

Zog nit kein-mol az du geist dem letz - tn veg.
pal-men land biz vai - tu land fun shnei,

Ven him - len blai - e - ne far shte - in bloi - e teg.
Mir ku - men on mit un - zer pain mit un - zer vei.

Ku - men vet noch un - zer ois - ge - benk - te sho,
Vu ge - fa - ln s'iz a shpritz fun un - zer blut,

S'vet a poik ton un - zer trot mir zai - nen do.
Shpro - tzn vet dort un - zer gvu - re un - zer mut.

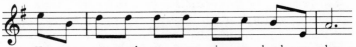

Ku - men vet noch un - zer ois - ge - benk te sho,
Vu ge - fa - ln s'iz a shpritz fun un - zer blut,

S'vet a poik ton un-zer trot mir zai - nen do. Fun gri-nem
Shpro-tzn vet dort un-zer gvu - re un - zer mut.

Narrator

We remember the six million by reciting the *Kaddish,* the traditional Jewish prayer for the dead.

This prayer is not a funeral hymn but an affirmation of God's everlasting Presence and dominion, praising God's existence and creative love. It is in this spirit that we pray the *Kaddish* remembering the victims of the Holocaust. We also pray for the survivors, whose faith in life enabled them to rebuild in other countries their shattered lives, their destroyed worlds. Joining together they brought about new life, they raised new families in new lands, in defiance of absolute terror and despair, an invincible hope. Exalted by that spirit of lifegiving and faith we pray today.

(The narrator or a reader familiar with Hebrew says or chants the *Kaddish*).

(Congregation stands)

יִתְגַּדַּל וְיִתְקַדַּשׁ שְׁמֵהּ רַבָּא בְּעָלְמָא דִּי־בְרָא כִרְעוּתֵהּ,

Yit-ga-dal ve-yit-ka-dash she-mei ra-ba be-al-ma di-ve-ra chi-re-u-tei,

וְיַמְלִיךְ מַלְכוּתֵהּ בְּחַיֵּיכוֹן וּבְיוֹמֵיכוֹן וּבְחַיֵּי דְכָל־בֵּית

ve-yam-lich mal-chu-tei be-cha-yei-chon u-ve-yo-mei-chon u-ve-cha-yei de-chol beit

יִשְׂרָאֵל, בַּעֲגָלָא וּבִזְמַן קָרִיב, וְאִמְרוּ: אָמֵן:

Yis-ra-eil, ba-a-ga-la u-vi-ze-man ka-riv, ve-i-me-ru: a-mein.

יְהֵא שְׁמֵהּ רַבָּא מְבָרַךְ לְעָלַם וּלְעָלְמֵי עָלְמַיָּא.

Ye-hei she-mei ra-ba me-va-rach le-a-lam u-le-al-mei al-ma-ya.

יִתְבָּרַךְ וְיִשְׁתַּבַּח, וְיִתְפָּאַר וְיִתְרוֹמַם וְיִתְנַשֵּׂא, וְיִתְהַדַּר

Yit-ba-rach ve-yish-ta-bach, ve-yit-pa-ar ve-yit-ro-mam ve-yit-na-sei, ve-yit-had-dar

וְיִתְעַלֶּה וְיִתְהַלַּל שְׁמֵהּ דְּקוּדְשָׁא, בְּרִיךְ הוּא, לְעֵלָּא מִן־כָּל־

ve-yit-a-leh ve-yit-ha-lal she-mei de-ku-de-sha, be-rich hu, le-ei-la min kol

בִּרְכָתָא וְשִׁירָתָא, תֻּשְׁבְּחָתָא וְנֶחֱמָתָא דַּאֲמִירָן בְּעָלְמָא,

bi-re-cha-ta ve-shi-ra-ta, tush-be-cha-ta ve-ne-che-ma-ta, da-a-mi-ran be-al-ma,

וְאִמְרוּ: אָמֵן.

ve-i-me-ru: a-mein.

יְהֵא שְׁלָמָא רַבָּא מִן־שְׁמַיָּא וְחַיִּים עָלֵינוּ וְעַל־כָּל־יִשְׂרָאֵל,
Ye-hei she-la-ma ra-ba min she-ma-ya ve-cha-yim a-lei-nu ve-al kol
Yis-ra-eil,

וְאִמְרוּ: אָמֵן.
ve-i-me-ru: a-mein.

עֹשֶׂה שָׁלוֹם בִּמְרוֹמָיו, הוּא יַעֲשֶׂה שָׁלוֹם עָלֵינוּ וְעַל־כָּל־
O-seh sha-lom bi-me-ro-mav, hu ya-a-seh sha-lom a-lei-nu ve-al kol

יִשְׂרָאֵל, וְאִמְרוּ: אָמֵן.
Yis-ra-eil, ve-i-me-ru: a-mein.

Reader

Hallowed and enhanced may God be throughout the
world. May God's sovereignty soon be accepted, during
our life and the life of all Israel. And let us say: Amen.

Congregation

May God be praised throughout all time.

Reader

Glorified and celebrated, lauded and praised, acclaimed
and honored, extolled and exalted may the Holy one be,
far beyond all song and psalm, beyond all tributes which
humanity can utter. And let us say: Amen.

Congregation

Let there be abundant peace from Heaven, with life's
goodness for us and for all the people Israel. And let us
say: Amen.

Reader

God who brings peace to the universe will bring peace
to us, to humanity, and to Israel. And let us say: Amen.

Congregation

Exalted, compassionate God, grant perfect peace in your
sheltering Presence, among the holy and the pure, to the
soul of all the men, women and children of the house of
Israel, to the Righteous Gentiles, to the millions who
died defending the right to be different, at a time of madness and terror.

May their memory endure, may it inspire truth

and loyalty in our lives, in our religious commitment and tasks. May their memory be a blessing and sign of peace for all humanity. And let us say all together: Amen.

(Congregation be seated)

Narrator
We end our worship by reciting together the words found on the walls of a cellar in Cologne, Germany, where Jews hid from the Nazis:

Narrator and Congregation
> I believe,
> I believe in the sun
> even when it is not shining.
> I believe in love
> even when feeling it not.
> I believe in God
> even when God is silent. *(A short period of silence)*

Narrator
We have proclaimed together our faith in the One God, Ground and Nurturer of us all. Before we go our separate ways again, let us extend to one another a sign of reconciliation expressing our hope for peace.

(Congregation stands)

Please turn to those around you, share the blessing of peace, wholeness, and life, and wish them Shalom!

Congregation
Shalom!

TO THE SIX MILLION

Authors' Biographies

ELIE WIESEL was born in Romania in 1928. He was deported with his family to Auschwitz when he was still a boy, and then to Buchenwald, where his parents and a younger sister were killed. *Night,* his first book, is the moving memoir of these experiences. After the war he moved to Paris, where he adopted the French language. His work as a journalist took him to Israel and finally to the United States.

Elie Wiesel has achieved an international reputation with such books as *A Beggar in Jerusalem,* which won the French Prix Medicis for 1969. *Souls on Fire* is a collection of portraits and legends describing the Hasidic masters who revitalized Judaism. *Somewhere a Master* is the sequel to that masterpiece. His other books are *Dawn, The Accident, The Town Beyond the Wall, The Gates of the Forest, The Jews of Silence, Legends of Our Time, One Generation After, The Oath, Ani Maamin: A Cantata, Zalmen, or the Madness of God, A Jew Today, Four Hasidic Masters, The Testament* (which was awarded the Prix-Inter for 1980), *The Fifth Son* and *Twilight.*

Elie Wiesel is Andrew W. Mellon Professor in the Humanities at Boston University. He is also Chairman of the U.S. Holocaust Memorial Council. He and his family live in New York City.

Elie Wiesel was awarded the Nobel Peace Prize in 1986.

ALBERT H. FRIEDLANDER was born in Berlin in 1927. He left Germany in 1939 and came to the United States via Cuba. He is a graduate of the University of Chicago and was ordained a rabbi by the Hebrew Union College, which also conferred upon him a Doctor of Divinity degree. He received his Ph.D. from Columbia University, where he acted as chaplain for Jewish students from 1961 to 1966. One of his books, *Never Trust A God Over*

Thirty, deals with the religious problems of university students. His pioneer work in Holocaust studies produced two major books: *Out of the Whirlwind* (1967), which is still in print as the definitive anthology of Holocaust literature, and *Leo Baeck: Teacher of Theresienstadt* (1968). Rabbi Friedlander served congregations in Arkansas, Pennsylvania, and East Hampton, N.Y. before moving to Great Britain. He is presently senior rabbi of the Westminster Synagogue and is the Dean of the Leo Baeck College, a progressive seminary ordaining European rabbis. He has lectured at many universities in Europe and the United States, and has published more than a hundred articles in scholarly journals, as well as books in the fields of theology, history and literature.

Rabbi Friedlander and his wife Evelyn live in London with their three children.